LEAVING A LEGACY WORTH LIVING

A Journey of Faith by a Woman
Who Doesn't Want to Die
with Her Song Still in Her

By
Barbara E. Howard

Copyright © 2012 by Barbara E. Howard

LEAVING A LEGACY WORTH LIVING
by Barbara E. Howard

Printed in the United States of America

ISBN 9781606475737

All rights reserved solely by the author. The author guarantees all contents are original and do not infringe upon the legal rights of any other person or work. No part of this book may be reproduced in any form without the permission of the author. The views expressed in this book are not necessarily those of the publisher.

Unless otherwise indicated, Bible quotations are taken from The NIV Serendipity Bible for Study Groups. Copyright © 1988 by Zondervan Publishing House.

www.xulonpress.com

Acknowledgments

This book would not have been possible without the love and support of family and friends. I especially want to thank my children Kelly, Mark and Ann, for taking this faith journey with me and providing hope when mine was almost gone. Their strength, belief in God, and belief in me has held me together through the worst and best of times. I am sharing the following stories for them, the dozen grandchildren they have blessed me with, and any others who might read this book. It is my prayer that everyone will understand why it it so important that they accept, believe, and follow the same God who sought me, caught me, and has held me for over 60 years. It is my greatest desire to spend eternity with all of you in the presence of our Lord and King, Jesus Christ.

I also want to thank the people at Single

Point Ministries of Ward Evangelical Presbyterian Church for their encouragement, faith and financial support as I walked the journey I never thought I would. Special thanks to Kathleen and Lisa, who pushed me in front of others to share my faith. And to Pastors Andy, Paul and Dick, who allowed it to happen. My group of spiritual sisters taught me the wisdom of belonging to a small group in order to stay sane in this often up-side down world. They are the "icing" on my cake.

Unbeknownst to most of them, but with the pastor's permission, I thank the congregation of the Congregational Church of the Villages, Florida. I was allowed to use our Ministry Center to get this book from my head into the computer. It was the perfect surrounding for me to accomplish something I couldn't seem to do at home. In addition to eliminating the distractions (of my own making at home), the center included a large table, good lighting, AC, a refrigerator, microwave, coffee pot, and even private bathroom. It was the perfect place for me to spend several hours over several days pounding a key board. Thank you so much.

To my Editors, Gail and Donna, *a very BIG thank*

Acknowledgments

you! They found several bloopers and helped me "clean it up good." Any errors you find are of my making, not theirs.

This book would not have been written without my loving, gracious, funny and patient husband of the last five years. Mike has supported me and allowed my dream to write my story become a reality. Why God has blessed me with him, I do not know. But I won't argue with Him about it! May He give us many fulfilling, loving, spirit-led years together.

I have said *no* to God in many areas of my life before I got wise enough to say *yes*. Writing this book is one of the ways I finally said *yes* to Him. So I dedicate it to my Heavenly Father and pray He is pleased.

> "Since my youth, Oh God, you have taught me, and to this day I declare your marvelous deeds. Even when I am old and gray, do not forsake me, O God, till I declare your power to the next generation, your might to all who are to come." Psalm 71:17-18

Introduction

To my precious grandchildren: Believe it or not, I used to be your age. I used to struggle with some of the same things you do. I went to school, did homework, fretted over pimples, got in trouble with my folks, learned to read, write and do the math. One thing I didn't do often was talk. When you don't speak, you spend a lot of time 'in your head': thinking, pondering, questioning and doubting. One of the things I wondered about was God. I received my first Bible when I was in the 3rd grade. I knew it was a special book, but wasn't sure what to do with it. I kept it by my bed, read it from time to time, but couldn't make much sense of it. However the stories I heard in Sunday school and at Vacation Bible School were very interesting to me. I remember how the teacher would use flannel boards and pieces of felt to tell Bible stories. (DVDs had not been developed yet.) It helped them to come alive for me. I particularly remember a large picture in our classroom of Jesus standing at a door with His hand posed to knock on it, but there was no handle on the door. It was to remind us that Jesus stands knocking at the door of our hearts, but the door must be opened on the inside, by us. *What did that mean?*

When I was about twelve, I was sitting in the choir loft watching the candle flames move with the air circulating in the church. And I did a very brave or very stupid thing. I said, *"God, if you are real, please blow out that candle."* Nothing happened. Immediately I felt guilty for asking the Lord of the universe, who has much more important things to do, to answer my silly request. Who was I to think He should do what I asked to prove His existence to me?

Our family went to church on a regular basis, but we didn't talk about God. On special holidays and some Sundays we would say grace before dinner. It was always the same one my parents had memorized in their homes while growing up.

Introduction

When my parents dropped me off at college, I remember my mother taking my hand and saying, "With God and you, anything is possible." It is the only time I remember my mom mentioning Him in a personal way.

I'm writing my story so that you will have a clearer picture of me, but more importantly, my journey with God. It has been long, difficult, scary and thrilling... but it has all been worthwhile and I'm hoping it will speak to you and help you on your journey with Him. For Bret, Montana, Desiree, Brandon, Kate, Angelica, Carson, Landon, Jake, Amanda, Josh and Quinn, that is my prayer for all of you.

If anyone else moves closer to God by reading this and asking important questions of themselves, I will consider it a double blessing.

Chapter 1

"Leaving a Legacy Worth Living"

Henry David Thoreau, well-known and respected author and naturalist, once said, "Most men live lives of quiet desperation and go to their grave with their song still in them." Another famous man, well known speaker and Creator, Jesus Christ, once said, "I have come that you may have life, and have it to the full." (John 10:10) So I wondered, *Why would most of us choose a life of quiet desperation when the Creator of the Universe offers us a LIFE IN ALL ITS FULLNESS?* I think it's because we ignore or to refuse to walk through special doors God has waiting for us. I believe all people can live a life with the richness and the fullness that Christ offers if we will walk through "The Door of Faith," "The Door of Gratefulness" and "The Door of Opportunity."

The first twenty-five years of my life were spent feeling guilty because I had done nothing to deserve my very good circumstances. I was born in America, white, female and free. The Lord gave me two parents who provided food, clothing, shelter, love and an education. They taught me manners and morals, fairness and fun. My body did everything it was supposed to do: I could see, hear, walk, talk, breathe, eat, sleep, think, feel, reason, laugh and cry. I also came to the realization that there had to be a much bigger power than my parents who provided all these things. Yet I never did anything to earn or deserve any of it, thus I felt guilty.

More years than I care to mention were spent dealing with the knowledge that I had received undeserved blessings from someone and would often ask *Why me?* I thought about African women who lived in huts, cooked over open fires, saw and smelled sewage running down the street, just feet from where they lived. They had possibly buried

Chapter 1

three of their six children before their children reached the age of two. These thoughts made we wonder, *If that had been my life, would I believe in a God who loved* and *cared for me?* It was easy to be a Christian in America in the 1940s and 1950s: be nice to people, share your stuff, go to church, be fair, don't cheat or swear, and do "all those other things we learned in kindergarten." Where would my faith be if I was raised in a third-world country? I pondered this question into my 20s when I received even *more* blessings: a husband who loved me, three healthy, beautiful children, and a lovely home in the country. How could this be? Wasn't it all a bit too much for one woman to have? Life was not perfect, but it was close enough.

Since then my faith has been tested again and again, and just when I thought I had Life with a capitol "L" all figured out, I found myself back at square one. It has taken me my whole life to learn that, whether in sickness or in health, for richer or for poorer, in the valleys or on the mountain tops, it is vital to our spiritual growth to walk through the three special doors I mentioned before. Walk through these Doors of Faith, Gratefulness and Opportunity that God has for everyone, and learn that they can make all the difference in your life.

Chapter 2

As a pre-teen, I started questioning the meaning of life. I thought there must be more to life than being born, growing up, getting a job, maybe getting married, having some children, watching them grow up and then dying. *Wasn't there?*

What prompted me to ask this question was seeing my father cry for the first time. Our dog Pokey, who was part of our family for at least ten years, had died. That afternoon Mom sent me to the basement to get something out of our freezer for dinner. I didn't want to go. I knew that Pokey was dead and lying on a newspaper down there. Other than mosquitoes, spiders, flies and wasps, I had never seen anything dead. On my way down the stairs, my father was coming up and he was crying. That shook me even more than Pokey's death. For the first time since hearing our dog had died, I fled to my room, threw myself on my bed and cried *Is this all there is?* Surely, if there was a God who had created us, there was more to life than living and dying. So I started my quest to find out more about Jesus and what He had to do with my life, if anything.

Our family went to church most Sundays, as their families had before. We were baptized as infants. Dad polished our Sunday shoes on Saturday night and we had our weekly showers on Saturday night too. (Yes, once a week showers seemed to work, as impossible as that probably sounds now.) Sundays were set aside to do things we normally didn't do during the week, i.e.: put on our "better" clothes, our Sunday shoes, go to church, say grace before dinner, have a nice dinner in the middle of the afternoon, and generally play quieter than we did on other days. We might have done homework, but we didn't do laundry or other house-hold chores on Sunday. On Good Friday, there was no school, but we had to go to our bedrooms and be quiet from noon to 3 P.M. because those were the hours that Christ

Chapter 2

was crucified. It was normal for us. I thought it was normal for everyone.

We considered our family Christian because of the things we were taught: respect God and other people, respect our property and others' property, be kind, polite, use your manners, pick up after yourself, and share with others. In other words, be good!

I spent most of my childhood doing these things, which made my sister and brother think our parents liked me better. Somehow keeping the peace and playing by the rules made more sense to me than bucking them and getting into trouble. I figured if I didn't say or do much, I couldn't say or do much that would cause problems. But, believe me, I was not perfect. In fact, I remember my mother saying, "If looks could kill, Barbara, you would have killed several people by now." Ouch! I must say, mom was the easier parent to please, so this was a pretty rough thing to hear from her. Our father was stricter, though I don't believe he was harsh. I stayed on his 'good side' as often as possible and found out years later that the neighborhood kids were afraid of him because of his stern look. Maybe they never saw him smile, which was beautiful when it happened.

These morals and manners, along with an unusual sense of guilt, carried me through my middle-school years, my high-school years, a couple of years in college and right into the arms of Mr. Tall, Dark and Handsome.

Carrying guilt continued to plague me because of the countless blessings I *kept* receiving. I had met Mr. Wonderful, fallen in love, gotten married, lived in a nice home, and was blessed with two perfectly healthy and beautiful children in our first three years of marriage. My all-time favorite dream of becoming a wife and mother was realized by the time I was 22. Life was good! It was *very good*! But still I wondered, *Why all this? And why me?*

Then a number of things happened over the next few years that blew my life apart. I was shocked to discover that playing fair, minding my manners, living a moral life and having a basic faith, couldn't hold me together when my world crashed. My picture-perfect life was dropped,

Chapter 2

stepped on, broken into a 1000 different pieces and thrown into a pit full of mud. This may sound a bit dramatic, but without the grace, mercy and healing of my Lord and Savior, I would have physically died at age 29, or mentally and emotionally died in my 30s, or spiritually died in my 40s. And yet, now in my sixth decade, I am very much alive in all these areas. Has my life been easy? Has it gone according to my plan? To put it mildly, *NOT!*

I've been in the pits and deep valleys so many times that I once said to God, "Please go pick on someone your own size." But He also has taken me to the mountain top over and over again. I wouldn't wish my life on an enemy, but I wouldn't trade it with anyone else either, because of the things He has taught me and the places He has brought me. But if I had known, like a guest on Focus on the Family once said, "I didn't know that the way up would be down," I might have thought about checking out some time before my life became a nightmare.

Chapter 3

The way down began in the first year of our marriage, which included both the best and the worst of times for me. I was perfectly happy being a wife and mother, modeling these roles after watching my mother for 20 years. Doing things "mom's way" seemed to work for her but, unfortunately, did not always work for me. Instead of expressing myself to my husband when our differences occurred, I stuffed my hurts and worries and pretended all was well. Somehow I had come to the conclusion that if I argued with him, he would stop loving me. I never realized how this poor way of thinking and living could physically attack one's body. I got sick the first year of our marriage, when our first child was just five weeks old. I suffered with an intestinal illness that came on and off over the next eight

Chapter 3

years. It frequently had me doubled over in pain and hunting for a bathroom wherever I went.

The doctor couldn't give me any reason for what was happening. But I do remember two questions he asked at my first visit: "Have you been out of the country lately?" and "Did you want to have your baby?" The first question was a definite "no" and the second was a resounding "yes!" Medications and watching my diet kept me in remission from time to time, but never cured me. I was also told, after three hospitalizations, that surgery was the only cure. But I was so young the doctors didn't want to do it. So I was sent home, again and again. That is until the summer of 1973 when I was back in the ER in tremendous pain with a temperature of 100. That isn't very high, but when I had been released from the hospital just two weeks before, my doctor had warned, "if you develop a temperature again, come right back in." This time my own doctor was on vacation so his replacement came to check on me. He said something I thought about later: "You don't look that sick, but if you truly *feel* that badly, I will admit you." Less than 24 hours later this internist and a surgeon I had never met entered my hospital room, sat down on opposite sides of the bed and took hold of my hands. (We all know that doctors sitting on the bed of a patient are a no-no and taking the hands of a new patient is rather rare, so I realized something must be different this time).

X-rays showed I needed surgery in a matter of hours. However the doctor said I was too sick and, ideally, should be sent home and "built up" in order to survive the operation. He also said that if I went home without the surgery, I would surely die in matter of days. My guts were a mess and ready to explode. Once they did, it would be all over for me. A few hours later I was wheeled into the operating room with the knowledge that it might be my last trip anywhere. As if I needed more bad news, I was also told that I might survive the operation, but die shortly thereafter due to numerous complications that could arise.

At the age of 29, not having faced death before, I discovered I wasn't all that interested right then either. But strangely enough, although I was left alone with this fateful news twirling around in my

Chapter 3

mind for two hours (waiting for my husband to come), I never screamed or cried, *"Not this, not now, oh please God, not me!"* I didn't think it was proper to bargain with God after He had given me so much.

At that time I didn't know we could have a personal relationship with Jesus Christ, although I believed with all my heart that He loved me. So that morning we had quite a chat, God and I. I thanked Him for all the blessings He had bestowed on me: a caring family, a loving husband and three babies hoped for since I was about five.

I told Him I'd never given any consideration to the fact that I might be blessed with children, but then not allowed to raise them. I really wanted to be their mom, but told God, "If you have a better plan for them, I will accept it." I even suggested that my sister would be a good woman to raise our children as she loved them dearly too. So I hoped she would marry my husband if I didn't survive the operation. (Anyone else ever offer God a suggestion on how to handle your problems?) I've discovered He doesn't really need our help and sometimes we have to thank Him for *not* doing what we suggested.

Unfortunately I believed God had a warehouse full of a specific number of blessings. If He gave me anymore, it would shorten His supply for someone else. I already knew I had received more than I deserved, so I hadn't asked Him to heal me during my years of sickness. Thankfully I have since learned that His "Warehouse of Blessings" cannot be depleted by anyone, not even me. Although there was so much about God I did *not* know, I didn't believe He was cruel. So I reasoned that if I survived the surgery, I would live. I didn't think He would carry me through the operation, giving my family hope, and then take my life a few days later. Doing the only thing I could when I regained consciousness, I thanked Him profusely for bringing me through. I thought the worst was behind me and life would be wonderful again.

Five days later another operation became necessary due to the complications the doctors had mentioned. I was in the Intensive Care Unit for a long time and even "went out of my head" for awhile, not recognizing my husband or even knowing if I was married. A therapist was called in and, after talking to me, informed my family

Chapter 3

that he didn't know if I would come out of it or not. One night after I was moved into a regular room, my roommate was moved down the hall, because I must have been creating quite a racket. I was being assaulted with horrific nightmares. During this time, I woke up once and discovered I had been put in a straight jacket. Another time I awoke to find my hands tied to the bed rails. I tried tapping S.O.S. messages by banging my wedding ring against the rails, although I haven't a clue about S.O.S. codes. In these nightmares, which were very real to me, I saw my parents and siblings tortured in ways I could never imagine. I believed the end of the world had come and the messages over the P.A. system were all in code to keep me confused. Sometimes when I awoke there was blood on my hands and feet. I was convinced that the devil came to me at night and taunted me by saying, "You want your family to die, don't you, to put them out of their misery? But they're not going to. Their torture will continue forever." Talk about feeling demon possessed! No wonder no one wanted to talk to me about these things after I went home.

Hooked to numerous tubes and monitors and other beeping, fluid-draining machines, I probably looked like someone from outer space. My arms looked like pin cushions because the doctor wanted blood drawn daily to see how I was doing. Only once during my long stay were our six- and eight- year old children allowed in to see me. I wanted to sit in a chair and look as 'normal' as possible. But the doctor said, "No, if they think you are well, they will wonder why you can't go home. And it will be a long time before you go home." So I stayed in bed, hugged them as tightly as they could stand, and watched Mark who discovered all the things my bed could do when the assortment of buttons were pushed. I thought Kelly needed a hair cut badly, but by the time I was released, her hair had grown long enough so she was able to do something with it. She kept growing it until it reached her waistline, possibly to spite me for keeping it short when she was younger. It might never have grown as long as she wanted if I had been home during that "growing out" stage, so Kelly was blessed a bit by my absence. My mother held our four-month-old daughter, Ann,

Chapter 3

outside the hospital window because infants weren't allowed inside at all. It was a wonderful gesture, but I was on the fourth floor so I couldn't see her very well and certainly couldn't hold her as my arms longed to do. Knowing a special bond develops between a mother and her child in the first few months of life, I was afraid Ann wouldn't know me when I finally was able to go home. Yet she was a real trooper and it didn't take long before we connected at my home-coming.

It was days after the initial surgery before the doctor said, "Maybe you're going to make it." I smiled, but didn't say what I was thinking. *I could have told you that some time ago, because God had reassured me that if I survived the surgery, I was indeed going to live.* I wasn't bold about my beliefs and sharing them out loud was something I just didn't do. I regretted this years later. It was almost two months before I went home, but I left the hospital knowing something I hadn't realized before: A good life does not consist of how much stuff you have, how much money you make, what type of house you live in, or what kind of car you drive. Life is about PEOPLE. Our relationships to each other and God are all that matter. I feel very sad for a nurse who said to me as I was leaving the hospital, "I would rather die than live as you are going to have to." How tragic that she didn't have people in her life to love and didn't know that life is a gift from God which should be treasured, no matter what.

Chapter 4

Several months before surgery, when I was pregnant with our last child, I was depressed but didn't know why. I thought of it later as "my winter of discontent." After Kelly and Mark went to school, I would crawl back in bed for a few hours and sleep to avoid thinking. I think I fooled people by acting as if everything was okay, because that was the Golden Rule: be kind, be polite, mind your manners and never say anything negative. As I said, I was far from perfect, but I did my best to live by these rules.

After delivering our third perfectly healthy baby and surviving the disease that had threatened to kill me, I determined that I would never be depressed again! How could that possibly happen? My life had been saved by our precious Lord; I had a loving husband and three fantastic kids that I would be able to raise; a lovely home and extended family who loved us; and a body that continued to do most of the things it had before: I could see, hear, feel, walk, talk and laugh; I could once again feed myself and brush my teeth. Even rolling over in bed without help was a gift because there were weeks when I couldn't. I learned to master walking upstairs again, something my feet and legs had forgotten how to do. Fall, beautiful fall, with its colored leaves and wonderful-smelling breezes was coming. I had been through a valley I never anticipated, but had come out on a mountain top. Rejoicing and being thankful were part of every day. I walked through the "Door of Gratefulness" and life was good once more.

These feelings lasted about six months and then the black hole opened up again. I berated myself for feeling depressed and told myself I had no right to feel this way. But in spite of all the blessings I had received, something wasn't quite right and I couldn't put my finger on it. One morning in church, however, our pastor did.

I was new to this church and didn't know anyone there. On this particular Sunday in

Chapter 4

February of 1974, the pastor gave a sermon that the church board had warned him not to give. It seemed the church was divided into two camps. The people in the congregation were on different sides of an issue and couldn't come to an agreement. (I've since learned that happens frequently in churches...the devil must enjoy it immensely when unity in God's body falls apart.) This church was growing in numbers and running out of space in their building. Some people wanted to put an addition on the current building and others felt that, if another church was needed, someone else should build it. The pastor told the congregation just how he felt about this, upsetting both sides I am sure. I didn't feel attacked, however, because I didn't know what the sides were or who was on either one.

Somewhere in his message the pastor talked about our "commitment to Christ." He said that if anyone in the congregation wanted to make a commitment to Him, they should come forward and kneel at the altar rail. I'm not sure why it hit me the way it did, but I don't think I'd ever heard this before. I sat there thinking for a minute and then said to God: *"I don't know what you want from me. For years I've tried figuring it out for myself, but I'm exhausted and I give up. If there is anything you want of my life, come and take it, because I quit."* And then, because I figured most of the congregation would do what our pastor suggested, I rose from my seat at the back, walked to the front of the sanctuary and got down on my knees. As I knelt, I slowly turned my head to the left and to the right and saw there was only one other woman kneeling at the railing. I was totally embarrassed. I felt like a fool. I prayed for God to open the floor and let me drop through. If I'd had any inkling that I would not be joined by scores of others, I never would have had the nerve to walk up that aisle in front of a hundred people.

Years later, I realized I had answered an "altar call." I'd never seen this in the churches I had attended since childhood. In going forward, I made a public announcement that I was giving my life, whatever was left of it, to Christ. I thank Him to this day that, in His wisdom, God blinded me to what anyone else was doing or *not* doing. I've learned that when we are truly focused on

Chapter 4

Jesus, what other people think and do doesn't matter much. Was my life peaches and cream after this? Much to my surprise, it was not. In fact I reached a low point and said to God: *"My life was easier before you came into it. Can't I go back to where I was before I turned my life over to you?"* I looked around for awhile and decided there was no place else to go, so I continued my journey with Him that would continue to take me down in order to bring me up.

Chapter 5

My first test of this new faith came when it seemed like we would have to file for bankruptcy. We were spending more money than my husband was making and his "get-rich-quick" schemes failed each time. Our bank was throwing us out because of the number of over-drafts we accumulated in less than a year. True to form, I thought it was my job to rescue us. I worked out a budget and took it to a credit union where we had an account and presented my "sure-to-succeed" plan if they would just give us one more loan to get out of the mess we were in. What a shock it was when they turned us down. I was thoroughly embarrassed at the thought I wasn't trusted. To them, my word wasn't good enough. They had all the proof they needed from our past experiences with bounced checks. (My husband felt that as

Chapter 5

long as we paid their fees, they wouldn't care... guess they were getting as tired of the extra paper work as I was). As was my custom, I fretted and worried for days wondering, *What will we do now? This plan was our only hope.*

After dealing with these feelings and emotions for a few days, I thought, *Wait a minute. You've turned your life over to God. It is now your job to pray and to handle our money as best you can, then lay this burden at the foot of the cross. God is in control. He has promised to take care of us. He will work it out somehow.* I stopped loosing sleep and getting stomach aches because my heavy load had been handed to Someone who promised that He was strong enough to carry it. That Christmas my husband received a bonus from work that allowed us to get out of debt. I smiled and thanked God for His faithfulness. Through this and many other situations, God continued to teach me that obedience to Christ can lead to peace no matter what our circumstances. Each and every day we get to choose whether to focus on our problems or on the One who is the Answer.

Five years later my husband announced that

he wanted to leave our marriage. Shocked and scared, I knew this certainly wasn't part of my master plan either! Yes, I wanted to raise our kids, but I never considered doing it without my husband. In fact, I was sure I couldn't.

My husband had accomplished most of his goals by this time. All but Number One eluded him: Becoming a millionaire by the time he was thirty-five. He worked very hard, overcame the "blue collar" image he didn't like, met the woman of his dreams, helped create some neat kids, had a home in the country on a few acres, and was rising in the corporate world where his salary kept growing. And then he discovered it wasn't quite enough. He agreed to try some marriage counseling, so I found a minister I felt we could talk to. On our first visit, this pastor told him that he would never have the life he wanted without God. On our way to the car after the appointment my husband said that he would try everything else before he would try God. In his mind, only weak people needed God. Although he never said it, I believe his thoughts ran something like this: "There must be something more, something

Chapter 5

better, that I don't have. I'm not getting it through the life I have now, so I will leave, go out into the world, and find what will truly make me happy." And so he left. I knew I had contributed to the failure of our marriage by not being open and honest about my feelings, and in other ways too, but I believed we would work through this difficult time and somehow both be better for it.

In the meantime, I cried until I felt empty. I felt like I used a life time of tears in a few short years. I prayed. I beat my fists. I pleaded with God to bring my husband back and believed He would do that. The God I had given my life to would not have let this man come into my life if He knew he was going to leave me, *would He?* It made no sense at all. And so I waited and waited and waited some more for my husband to return. I counted the days, the weeks, the months and then the years.

Chapter 6

After three years of wallowing in self-pity because I was divorced *and* a single mom, I woke up to the fact that I better learn how to live the life that was now before me instead of waiting for my previous one to return. It was heartbreaking. It was against everything I ever wanted to do and every dream I'd had about what my life would be like. But it was time to accept the cards I had been dealt and play them. Then God used our youngest child to speak words of wisdom to me that could only have come from Him.

It was a warm, sunny day in the middle of summer and Ann, who was six by now, asked if she could get our mail. It sounds like a simple request, doesn't it? But our mailbox was across the road, about 350 feet away. She would have to walk down our long driveway, lined with trees, and

Chapter 6

cross the dirt road where she would be out of my sight. We lived in the country and you wouldn't think there could be much danger in doing that. But because of the numerous trees and limited number of houses, some people drove extremely fast, thinking no one was around and they could get away with it. In addition to cars, tractors, trucks, motorcycles and horses raced down our street. It wasn't exactly a safe place for a little girl. But I also knew that children don't grow up if we don't allow them to do things they've never tried before. So I said yes after giving her all the warnings a good mother should: "Look both ways before you cross the street; use your eyes, and use ears, *before* you use your feet." Ann skipped happily away, finally allowed to do something that only her 14-year-old sister and 12-year-old brother had previously done.

As soon as she was out the door, I went back to my sewing project. I cut, pinned, stitched and forgot about Ann and her mission. Sometime later Kelly came into the kitchen and asked if I had seen Ann lately. I jumped from my chair as my stomach leaped to my throat and went tearing out of the house. I ran as fast as possible until I could see her standing across the road. I calmed down a bit as she seemed to be all right. But I couldn't understand why she was just standing there, holding the mail. I cupped my hands and yelled, "Are you okay?" She nodded. "Do you need some help?" She nodded again. Realizing she wasn't hurt, I slowed my pace. *How could you, Barbara? How could you send her out here and then forget about her? Since your marriage didn't work, you have tried very hard to be a perfect parent. Boy, did you blow it today.* (I've since learned there is no such thing as a perfect spouse or perfect parent, try as we might).

Sure enough, Ann had kept her vigilance at the side of the mailbox. I noticed a mud puddle in front of the box and Ann's arms full of muddy envelopes. I asked her what happened and she explained, "I was getting the mail out of the box but had to step over this mud puddle to reach it. When I turned around to come back to the house, I dropped a piece in the mud. When I bent over to pick it up, I dropped another one and when I reached for that, another one fell out of my

Chapter 6

hands. After trying two or three times to get it all, I realized I wasn't getting anywhere so I waited for you to come and help me." I have no idea how long she had been there because I had gotten so wrapped up in my sewing. But surprisingly, she didn't yell at me. She wasn't screaming or crying. She was just standing there quietly waiting for my help. She believed with her whole heart that I loved her and would eventually come and help her out of her predicament. She ended her story with a smile and said, *"I knew it...I knew you'd come."*

I hugged her, took some of the mail and we started back to the house. About half-way back, I stopped. It felt like I had walked into a brick wall. And for the first time in my memory, God spoke to me. I didn't hear an actual voice. It was just thoughts coming at me very quickly that I never could have thought on my own. The one-sided conversation went something like this: "You think, Barbara, that I am ignoring your situation as a single mom. I know you made a promise to yourself back in high school that if you ever had kids they would never come home to an empty house. You had experienced that and didn't like it one bit. Now you realize you need to find a full-time job in order to make ends meet. That means your kids will be home alone for 2-3 hours after school before you get home from work. I realize this was never in your plan and you have been fighting with Me about this issue for some time. I would like to use this experience with Ann to let you know I will *never* forget or ignore your needs. You think I haven't heard your prayers. You're mad at Me for allowing this to happen. I need you to know that I love you even more than you love your children (which we both know is bucketloads). I have promised to provide and protect you, but you feel I've gotten too busy elsewhere. You feel pieces of your life falling into a mud puddle and are helpless to get them clean and put back together again. Please know that I am coming to help you. Believe that I love you too much to let this heart-ache persist in you forever. Please do what your six-year-old just did. Do all you know how to do, then stand and wait for me as patiently as Ann waited for you. And when I come, I want to hear you say to Me what Ann said to you with a smile and a look of confidence, *"I knew it...I knew you'd come."*

This conversation only took a matter of seconds, yet the lesson I learned helped me for a very long time. When I would get scared, I would remember this incident. It not only allowed me to survive those years as a single parent, it allowed me to grow and thrive in the process.

We walked the rest of the way to the house. I was so thankful that Ann was okay but also in shock that God had used this ordinary situation to speak volumes to me. I had been arguing with God that He must have confused me with someone else if He thought I could raise these kids without my husband in my life. But I finally had to realize that the Lord of the Universe believed I could do this. *He must know me better than I know myself.* It was time to throw off my mourning clothes and get busy being the best I could be with the life I had. Oh the countless experiences He has given me since then to prove over and over again just how real and faithful He is!

I did find full-time work that fall where I was respected, trusted and appreciated. It felt very good to be treated that way. In this family-owned business, I was eventually asked to do tasks that only the owners had done previously. This did much for my self-esteem. I often rode a roller-coaster of feelings because I enjoyed it so much, yet also felt guilty that my kids were left alone so often. It was difficult to manage and make peace with these conflicting feelings.

Chapter 7

Where was my church during this dark time of my life? For over a year, I didn't tell anyone that my husband had left. No one asked about him either because he hadn't attended church with us. I smiled every week as if all was well, never letting them know I was dying inside. I hid my secret because I feared their judgment rather than trusting them for support, something I'd been guilty of when thinking about divorced people. I thought divorced women wore bright red lipstick, fish-net stockings and plunging neck lines. They certainly didn't look like me! One day a woman invited our family to their home for lunch. It was time for me to share that my husband no longer lived with us. She got a rather puzzled look on her face and said, "Oh." And that was that. The invitation was dropped and we were never invited again. If you have any desire to minister to widows and orphans (which single parents and their kids are), a Sunday dinner invitation would do much to bolster and encourage them that they are still viable and valuable as a family.

A few years later, when I felt pretty healed, I volunteered to be a greeter at church Sunday mornings. The woman in charge said, *"Thank you, but we'd rather present a family image. You do understand, don't you?"* It felt like another knife had been jabbed through my heart when she said this. Thankfully not everyone treated me like a leper. Most folks just didn't know what to do with this "broken family," so they did nothing. Also, thankfully, there were a few that walked along side of us either by calling several times a week to assure me I could make it, or inviting "just the four of us" to their home for picnics and canoe rides. One family even asked my son to help out with their horses and farm work so Mark would have some healthy, male-bonding time. (Being raised in a household of females doesn't always help a boy become a man). I had failed to realize that the church consists of ordinary people: Non-perfect

Chapter 7

people, some with more in-sight, wisdom and understanding than others. It's unfair for any of us to blame the whole church when someone says something that tears us apart. Hopefully the things that happened to me, both the painful and the helpful, have improved my character and the way I treat others dealing with a loss of any kind.

Chapter 8

My years as a single parent were the most difficult yet most profound I ever had. I learned more about our kids, God and myself than at any other time. There were financial and emotional struggles yet to overcome. There were also blessings yet to be counted. I discovered that many areas of my life still needed to be released into His care. I read books, listened to tapes, Christian music and Christian radio (which I previously didn't know existed). I clung to special verses from the Bible by writing them on index cards and placing them in my surroundings wherever I could: taped to mirrors, stuck in cabinets, the car visor and my purse. When I didn't think I could put one more foot in front of me, I went to these verses and songs to remind myself Who was in control of my life. Verses like

Chapter 8

"being confident of this, that He who began a good work in you will carry it on to completion until the day of Christ Jesus" were anchors for my wobbly faith. The lyrics of "He Didn't Bring Us This Far" by Johnny Hall confirmed the above verse found in Philippians 1:6 and went round and round in my head, bringing me hope: "I didn't build my home in you to move away. I didn't teach you to swim to watch you drown. I didn't bring you up to let you down. I didn't bring you this far to leave you." God hadn't brought me this far to leave me? Oh what a comforting thought. I knew God had come into my life and these songs, Bible verses and other great quotes helped me keep my head above water...and my commitment to try and keep walking wherever God led me.

During this time when I felt I was riding a roller coaster through life, I read <u>Hinds Feet in High Places.</u> God used this allegory by Hannah Hurnard to assure me that my life was not unique and that others had also taken two steps forward and three steps back. I related totally to "Miss Much-Afraid," the main character. The Loving Shepherd in this story accompanied Much-Afraid on her journey from the Village of Much-Trembling to the High Places. God gave me the same traveling companions of Pain and Suffering that the Loving Shepherd had given her. It took a long time for both of us to accept the fact that 'the way up was down'. Much-Afraid fought it as hard as I did. Her misconceptions about God's character were as confused as mine. Yet, eventually, He led both of us to the mountain top where we basked in His presence, love, beauty and peace.

Much-Afraid was transformed into Grace & Glory when she reached the mountain top. Her traveling companions, Pain & Suffering were now called Joy & Peace. When Much-Afraid tried to thank them for sticking with her through all her struggles, they said "No, it is we who thank you. We couldn't have been transformed unless you had taken our hands and let us, as Pain & Suffering, help and guide you. Don't you know that everything that comes to the High Places is transformed?" We all wanted to stay on the mountain top with Him. But the time came when He said, "Yes, it is more wonderful here than you ever imagined, but I need you to go back down the

Chapter 8

mountain. There are still many hurting, lonely, sick, scared people in the valleys below and I want you to go and help them discover the way up here. It is lovely here, but I need you down there." So we went, knowing He would go with us. It was the "beginning of a new song for Grace & Glory, Joy & Peace," and thankfully, it was a new beginning for me too. Have you been struggling with God's purpose for your life over and over again? I highly recommend <u>Hinds Feet in High Places</u>, the Bible, and other books written by those who have met Him and had their lives transformed by Him.

Chapter 9

I worked full time for four years as an Office Manager, during which time my kids came home to an empty house every day after school. They were also on their own five days a week during the summer. The older two were too young to be raising their seven-year-old sister, but that is what happened, as I couldn't afford child-care. I still wanted desperately to return to being more involved in their lives. Kelly was in college, Mark was in high school and Ann was still in elementary school when I realized that before long, my years of investing in their lives on a regular basis would be over. I read the local papers looking for a job that would coincide with the school calendar. I wanted to be a school secretary, a bus driver, or work in the cafeteria. I was willing to sweep the floors, just so I could be

Chapter 9

home when they were. Again I was back on my knees before God. *Please help me find a way to return to their daily lives.*

However, working full time, managing a home, raising three children, doing the shopping, the banking, the errands, serving at church and being a chauffeur for the family, left little time for looking for another job. After much searching with no results, I resigned myself to stay where I was and be grateful I had a job I liked. I needed the appreciation, respect and, of course, the pay checks. As I mentioned, some days I felt guilty for enjoying my job when in my heart I really wanted to be "just a mom." To this day, I believe being a mom is the most important job in the world.

After accepting that I had to keep my full-time job to make ends meet, I was driving home one day when the Lord spoke to me again. I was thinking about how much full-time work was keeping me away from my children when I heard, "You can quit your job." Of course, I argued with that thought. *No I can't! I have three kids to raise, a mortgage and car loan to repay, and many other financial responsibilities.* (Even though my former husband sent support, for which I was very thankful, it was not enough.) I reinforced my argument with, *How can I possibly quit my job without any prospects waiting in the wings?* God replied, "Do you trust Me or don't you?" What a shocker that was! Yes, of course I trusted Him, but obviously God was not fully aware of my situation or He wouldn't ask such a thing of me. To which He replied, "Do you trust Me or don't you?"

I have since realized that if we only do things where we feel confident, capable and secure, how and where is God supposed to work in our lives? I once heard a woman at a conference say, "If I get an idea that is smarter than I am, it must be God speaking to me." That is the smartest and clearest definition of how God speaks to people than anything else I have heard. I would never have thought of quitting my job without another one waiting for me, so this idea must have come from God.

After praying and sharing this idea with the kids, Mark said, "If you believe that is what God wants you to do, then do it. We will be okay." Oh, the faith and trust of a child! So, against all odds

Chapter 9

and knowing I only had enough money to carry us for about two months, I turned in my resignation and went home to fulfill my dream of being a mom.

Chapter 10

It was November of 1984 and I knew I couldn't just sit in a chair and wait for God to drop a job in my lap that would work with the kids' school hours. So I wrote an ad for the local paper and listed myself as a Santa helper. I was available to shop for gifts, address Christmas cards, wrap presents, help decorate homes, etc. I'd even bake their Christmas cookies. Some people at my church thought it was a clever ad. No one hired me however. *Okay, now what?*

I had cleaned houses, while working part-time as our church secretary, before looking for full-time work, so decided to try that again. In time, I had enough customers to keep us afloat. I was even hired at the local clinic and received $450 a month to keep their offices clean. Ann came and helped in the evening or on weekends when she

Chapter 10

could. I could set my own hours and work my schedule around the kids' activities. My dream of being home was working. I didn't have health insurance or any other financial benefits during this time, but I was thrilled to once again have more time with my kids and be available for other events. One day while I was scrubbing a toilet, I said to God, "*although no job You ask me to do is beneath me, will a day come when You have something other than this in mind?*" What a surprise He had waiting for me (although it was over a year before He revealed it).

Jesus supplied everything we needed while I was self-employed. I didn't get sick and we all learned how to live on a budget. The kids can tell you today about the times we were able to go McDonald's and they knew they could either have a small hamburger and a milk shake or a bigger burger and a soda, but they couldn't have a big burger and a shake at the same meal because of the expense. Did we suffer through these financial 'hardships'? Not one bit. One day when I said I couldn't afford something, however, Ann said, "Just write a check." I realized then that more lessons were needed about handling money in the real world.

God used this time to teach me other lessons too. (Since I worked alone, there was a lot of time for thinking, listening and processing). As a teenager, I had baby sat for our pastor's son. I would listen as he and his wife took their baby's hands and prayed out loud over him before they left for the evening. I couldn't understand why they did this, since the child was much too young to understand anything they were saying. Now, as a single mom, the voice that came to me from time to time said, "It's time for you to start praying *with* your children, not just *for* them." Never having prayed aloud, and having no desire to start now, I tried to talk this thought out of my head. I used excuses like, *when they're older, or when they graduate from school or get their first job or when they get married or have a child, I'll pray with them then.* None of my excuses worked with God. Instead I heard, "If you don't start now, you never will." Sounded a bit like a threat to me, one I didn't want to believe. But in obedience to this command which could only come from God, I started praying with each child as I tucked them

Chapter 10

in at night. Like other things that were new to me, I was scared and my voice shook. I finally got the hang of it and realized we don't need to change our voice or our personalities to pray. God would like us to pray in the same tone, inflection and honesty as if we were talking to a dear friend who is in the room with us. (Which we really are). And although it was very difficult to start doing, it turned out to be some of my favorite and most blessed moments. Deciding that if five minutes on my knees holding their hand was good, ten minutes would be better, they occasionally said, "Could you make it shorter tonight, please?" I guess they grew weary of my prayers for the whole world. Did these prayers transport my children into the Kingdom of God? No, but I believe they helped them as they surely helped me. (Added bonus: it is now years later and they all pray with their children. It seems to come naturally to them and I am so thankful that it does). Even though my kids were *years* from getting married, I also prayed during this time that God would bring Godly spouses into their lives. When it was right, God brought Steve, Rich and Sue...all of whom have added blessing upon blessing to our family.

One week in July of 1985, while my mother was undergoing chemotherapy treatments, my father had a stroke. That same week, my only boyfriend since the divorce decided it was time he look elsewhere for the woman of his dreams. I assumed that I received three heavy blows at once because if they had come one at a time, I would have fallen apart. As it was, there wasn't any time for that. Hospitals, lawyers, social workers, the V.A., phone calls, appointments, taking mom for her chemo treatments at a hospital in one city and to another hospital in another city to visit dad, along with managing my own household, were *only* possible because my cleaning jobs allowed me to set my own schedule. If I had been working 9-5, five days a week, I have no idea how I could have handled these other situations. Let's face it. I couldn't have. As the Bible tells us, "The Lord will indeed give what is good...and prepares the way for his steps." (Psalm 85:12-13) I thanked Him for His insight and wisdom in preparing me two years ahead of time to be where I needed to be at this time. Who, but God, could have orchestrated that?

Chapter 11

A year later, the clinic where I received the largest portion of my income, canceled my contract. *Okay, Lord, what's next?* It "just so happened" (yeah, right) that in the fall of 1986 I was attending programs at a church that had a ministry for single adults. I had been through their Divorce Recovery Program, which taught me many things I needed to know. I was now facilitating groups in this program.

One evening after a circle prayer with our Divorce Recovery groups, the pastor to the single adults approached me and asked what I did for a living. When I informed him that I cleaned toilets, he told me he needed a secretary and would I please apply. I was shocked and surprised. He had no idea I had any secretarial experience or office skills. Again I wondered *"why me?"* I talked to God all the way home and explained to Him all the ways this job would not work: I had just moved to a city that was thirty minutes from this church (I was used to getting to my jobs in five to fifteen minutes); I still had house cleaning commitments; I was also a care-giver for a diabetic woman two to three times a week. I helped this lady with some basic needs and also provided companionship when she would otherwise be alone. We developed a neat bond, and although she could appear to be a crusty old lady at times, we shared a lot of laughs and got along just fine. I had grown to love her. How could I leave her now? As I rustled with these questions, I also reminded myself that the starting salary at the church was *less* than I was making at my odd assortment of jobs before the clinic canceled me. It didn't make any sense at all for me to take this job at the church.

The pastor had told me to pray over the weekend and come back Monday morning to take their employee entrance test, so I did. I did so more out of curiosity than anything else. For the first and only time in my life, I typed fifty words a

Chapter 11

minute without any errors. I took these amazing results as a sign from God that I was to take this new job. The pastor said he would try to get me more money and that I could continue to be a care-giver for Mildred once a week. I could also clean one house before coming to work to supplement my income. I tried doing all three jobs, but discovered after a few weeks that I just couldn't physically manage. So I quit the cleaning job and found a replacement to help Mildred. We both cried when I said good-bye.

When it was time to start this new job, my home situation had changed a great deal. My father had died, my mother was through with her chemo treatments, Kelly was in her last year of college, Mark had graduated from high school and was working out-of-state with his uncle, and Ann was a responsible teenager. Although I had no way of knowing it at the time, this job working with single adults would open a whole other world for me. Miracle of miracles, it also offered a place in ministry I had never contemplated. Prior to this, my cowardly out-look on life had decided that if I hadn't done something by my early thirties, I would probably never do it. I had no idea that a new Barbara was coming out of her cocoon and would start to fly like never before!

Chapter 12

Twice a month the ministry would bring in a speaker to talk on a topic of interest to single adults. Our ministry consisted of people who were divorced, widowed and those who had never married. A few months after joining the staff, the inner voice (which by now I was sure was God) told me that I should give one of these talks. As with every other difficult situation He had asked me to face, I said, *"No way. Once again, you have me confused with someone else. You know I don't speak in public. In case you've forgotten, I'm the one who had no desire to be a teacher because they had to stand in front of a group and talk, and I just didn't do this. Surely you can find someone else to give this talk."*

God then proceeded to remind me of three specific things that had happened and how He had spoken to me through them. That was the gist of it. After months of His badgering, my arguing, and losing sleep over it, I finally said, *"Okay, okay, I will do this one talk and then please leave me alone."*

The night came. About one hundred people showed up. With my stomach tied in knots, my hands sweating, my feet freezing and my mind screaming, *"Why did you say yes to this?"* I approached the podium and held on tightly. I had been writing my thoughts for years, so I was prepared with a word-for-word typed script. I read it. I tried to remember to look at the audience once in awhile. All I remember was reading the last line of my script, thanking them for their attention, walking to the back of the room and collapsing in a chair with relief. It was over and I would never have to do it again! What peace, what joy flooded my heart.

A few minutes later people approached me and said, "You spoke from your heart and touched mine." "I have to give a talk next week. Will you give it for me?" "Thank you so much, you really ministered to me." I gulped, tried to find my voice

Chapter 12

and explained that, no, I was not a speaker and no, I hadn't any intention of speaking in public again. Little did I know that this was the beginning of a ministry that would teach me more than I ever taught about the Man who had been holding my hand since the beginning of time.

Eventually, I spoke not only at our ministry functions, but also had speaking engagements outside our church. The first time I did that was at a church where Patsy Clairmont, nationally known Christian speaker, author and very funny lady, was the main guest. I would be doing a workshop for single ladies. It was an honor and I shook with excitement and also with fear. Before it was time for my workshop to begin, one of their committee members handed me an envelope and said that in case she didn't see me afterward, they wanted to thank me for coming. When the seminar was over, I went to my car and opened the envelope. It was a note saying how good I had been, thanking me for my time and also included a check for $40.00! Wow...my first honorarium... what a thrill! The fact that the lady had thanked me for my "good" talk *before* I spoke made me laugh. I smiled all the way home.

Our ministry decided to start a four-day vacation for single parents and their children. I was asked to do the workshops and was pleased to present four or five topics that I thought would be of interest to them. The pastor commented after my first message, "Wow, you really prepared for this, didn't you?" (He did well as a preacher, but was very comfortable 'winging it'... something I didn't dare try). Unbelievably I had gone from "how can I fill up five minutes?" to "how can I get it all in with only four days to share the pains and joys of being a single parent?" In between times, I occasionally filled in for our pastor who taught a class on Sunday mornings to 200-300 single adults. I became known as the "basket lady" because I usually had several props with me to illustrate my point. I still had pages of notes, sweating palms, freezing feet and a jumping stomach, but after the first few minutes, I usually settled down and let God do His thing through me.

After a few years of enduring the queasy stomach and pains that accompanied me each time I spoke, I said to God, *"if I am to speak for*

Chapter 12

You, couldn't You please take away all the discomfort I go through ahead of time?" His always-wise response? "If I take away your discomfort, you will start believing that is it you who are teaching these people when we both know that without Me you could do none of this. I'm just using your mouth and personality to reach them." Then and there I decided to let my discomfort be used for His glory. So now when the devil taunts me shortly before I speak with, "your points don't connect, they won't get it, just who do you think you are to speak for God?," I remind the bad guy *and* myself that God will be with me and carry me through. And, true to His word, He does. I will make peace with the pain as long as it keeps me depending on the Prince of Peace. If I ever stop being real or speaking the truth in His name, I hope someone yanks me off the platform.

I continue to stand amazed at the things the Lord has allowed me to experience, both the good and the ugly, and thank Him for loving me so much. At one point, I was ready to quit on Him. At another, I was able to sincerely say, "Though He slay me, yet will I hope in Him." (Job 13:15)

What have I to fear? Whether I live or die, I will be with Him.

I have had the privilege to stand before a group of single adult leaders across the country and make them laugh with my antidotes and stir their thinking with my thoughts. I did the Single Parent Vacations for ten years and several Women's Retreats. As I got older, so did the people in our ministry. I found we had a lot of grandparents who, like me, didn't get enough quality time with their grandchildren, so I planned and executed Grandparent-Grandchildren Vacations. They were a hit with both generations and have continued years after I retired. Oh, the special memories I have stored in my heart and recorded in my photo albums of those times I got to spend with my grand-kids. *Thank you, God, for each and every one.*

Chapter 13

*B*efore I began to speak to others about my faith, I had read that God gives gifts to each of His children. (Previously I had decided that I must have been home sick when He passed them out, because I couldn't think of anything special I could do). A few years into speaking to my Sunday morning class, I was thinking about some gifts I had received over several years and how I reacted to them. So I wrote a message titled "Did You Get the Gift You Wanted?" I wanted the class to reflect on whether we felt the same about the gifts we received from family and friends as the gifts we receive from God. Following are some of the thoughts I shared:

What is a gift anyway? Something freely given, freely received. If it comes with strings attached, it really isn't a gift. How often do we receive "just what we wanted, just the right color, just the right style" and most important, "just the right size?" Most of the gifts I have received were made with love or bought with care; some came beautifully wrapped, some were wrapped in newspaper. But sometimes because of the choice of the gift or the giver themselves, I didn't appreciate the love and thought put into these particular gifts. I certainly didn't receive them the way the giver had anticipated. I remember particularly the following three gifts because of the feelings and emotions they evoked in me.

My love of writing started when I was about nine years old. My grandmother, who had been widowed a year or two, moved to California and asked that we write letters to her. Writing was something I liked to do and, even though my life was about as exciting as watching a worm crawl through grass, I wrote something to her. My parents shared she had written to them and said, "I just love getting Barbara's letters." It is my earliest recollection of a compliment—so I hung on every word—and kept on writing. We had a typewriter in our house that had belonged to my other

Chapter 13

grandmother that was made in the early 1900's, I am sure. It didn't work very well and I remember dreaming of having a new one—one that typed each letter clearly. (Of course today I wish I still had that old Royal typewriter—it's probably worth a mint!)

Christmas came right on time and it was our family's habit (after everyone knew who Santa was) to put our gifts under the tree before we went to bed on Christmas Eve. Naturally, as kids, we looked them over pretty good! Much to my delight and surprise, there was a box under the tree about the size of a typewriter and it had my name on it! Now, next to writing, my second favorite hobby was sleeping in—and Christmas morning had never been an exception. But since my brother and sister were always more anxious, they usually woke me about 6AM with whispers of, "It's time! Barbara *wake up. It's time!*"

Contrary to my usual sleeping-in habits, I don't think I slept more than 15 minutes that particular Christmas Eve. In my mind I had opened and reopened that box all night so I thought, "How am I going to act surprised when I open my gift of a new typewriter? I don't want to disappoint my parents and ruin the surprise they planned for me, so I'll have to be a very good actress in the morning." Well, I needn't have worried. Because when I truly opened the box, I discovered that the contents resembled a typewriter as much as a sparrow resembles a giraffe. The surprised look on my face was not the result of any acting. The box contained a white, plastic filigree ball that you could fill with artificial flowers as a decoration. (Like I said---as much like a sparrow looks like a giraffe). My parents meant well---so I acted as if all *was* well; I accepted their gift, but my disappointment went very, very deep.

When I was in the 6th grade, I received my first box of chocolates from a boy on Valentine's Day. I should have been thrilled, right? But when he brought the gift to our front door, I took it, mumbled a quick 'thank you', closed the door in his face, and hid the candy under my bed. Not exactly the best response from a "nice girl" who loved chocolate, was it? It was the giver this time that was my problem. I didn't want anyone to know this boy had given me something because

Chapter 13

it would have been embarrassing if anyone found out he liked me. Why? Because he was probably the most ridiculed boy in our school. Each morning we waited at the same bus stop with a gang of other kids from the neighborhood. The kids teased him, called him names, and made jokes about him. They were down-right cruel. My mother had taught me to be nice to everyone, however, so I didn't join in the teasing, and besides, I felt sorry for him. I was probably the only one who talked to him and treated him like a normal person. He was teased because he had two very big strikes against him: he probably weighed close to 200 lbs. at ten years of age and his name was Hildrith. (*Hildrith, if you're out there, I apologize for not doing anything to make the other kids stop their harassment. I pray the adult world has been kinder to you than we were*). I accepted Hildrith's gift, but hid it because I was embarrassed by it.

I loved the third gift I remember receiving that created lasting feelings. My son and his wife were moving to Florida, and she gave me her beautiful, lined, honest-to-goodness real black leather gloves---saying with a smile, "I won't need these anymore". I wore those gloves with great joy and thankfulness and, for the first time in years, my hands stayed warm despite our winter weather. The following year, when I started rounding up boots, scarves, mittens, and winter coats (you know, the usual stuff people in the northern states need every winter), those wonderful gloves were nowhere to be found. I hunted high and low, every place I could think of where they might be and several places where I was sure they weren't, and sure enough, they weren't. I suffered that winter with my usual knitted mittens and cold hands, sick that I had lost this precious gift. The next fall, with winter approaching and knowing that warm hands were possible as long as you have the right gloves, I started pricing real leather gloves. I laughed. I cried. I even thought about taking out a loan and making monthly payments. I had no idea that any pair of gloves could cost more than $50.00.

As I started rounding up my usual pile of items needed for winter, I found my previously-lost gloves right on the top shelf of my coat closet!

Chapter 13

That didn't make any sense to me since I had torn that closet apart the previous fall. What a blessing to find them! I had accepted these fabulous gloves, put them away for a season, and then thought they were lost forever.

Thinking about how I treated and reacted to these gifts, (the box of chocolates, the filigree ball and the pair of leather gloves), got me to thinking about God's gifts to us and how we feel, or don't feel, about them.

Just like any good father, God has given gifts to each of us. When we don't think we've been gifted in any way, we discount God's Word because it says we have! And just like the people who gave me gifts and expected me to use them, God expects us to use the gifts He has given us. "There are different kinds of gifts, but the same Spirit. There are different kinds of service, but the same Lord. There are different kinds of working, but the same God works all of them in all men. All these are the work of one and the same spirit, and He gives them to each one, just as He determines." (I Corinthians 12:4 & 11) The Living Bible says it like this: "It is the same and only Holy Spirit who gives all these gifts and powers, deciding which one each of us should have."

Imagine that! The same God who made us, who knew us before we were born, who gave us certain temperaments and personalities, also chose specific gifts for us to help Him bring the Good News to people. He doesn't gift us so we can keep our gifts hidden either. Quite the contrary... we receive specific, hand-picked gifts so we can live the abundant life He wants for us and help to build the Kingdom of God here on Earth.

He left His mission with a hand-full of very ordinary people who shared it with those they met, who shared it with everyone they could, who shared it with the next generation, who handed it down to the *next* generation. Thank goodness that, no matter how many times the world has tried to snuff out His Word and His story, it has been preserved through countless generations so we could know it too. Everyone needs this Savior and Lord. To honor Him and those who came before us, often at risk to their very lives, how can we drop the ball now?

We need to realize that God has gifted all His

Chapter 13

children for a reason, and I believe, for a season. *For a season?* Does that mean He'll take it back if we don't use it? I think He might. Imagine you have a child. You feel you know him very well. After all, you raised him, watched his temperament, tried to train it at times, and had observed his likes and dislikes. So, after much thought, you select what you feel is the perfect gift for his birthday.

After he opens your gift and gives a perfunctory "thank you", he takes it to his bedroom and puts it at the back of his closet. Days go by, weeks go by, months go by…the gift is now dusty and a spider has spun a marvelous web on it. How many of us would wait that long before we'd go into his closet, grab the gift, shake it in front of him and say, "If you're not going to appreciate and use this, I'll give it to someone who will!" Wouldn't that be the most expected, natural thing to do? Just like God's gifts, what good is any gift if we keep it in the back of our closet?

The store-bought or hand-made gifts we receive may disappoint or embarrass us. They may be the wrong size, the wrong color, or even something we wouldn't be caught dead wearing or have in our home. Yet that will never happen with our gifts from God. We needn't boast about our gifts, in fact we can't. How can we boast about something we didn't ask or work for? All we can boast about is the giver...whether that is a parent, a child, a spouse, a friend, and even the Creator of the Universe.

Chapter 14

*O*nce I knew that all God's promises are true for all of us, I decided I didn't want to be ignorant about what my gift might be. So after discovering there was a test that would help show us what our gifts were, I decided to take it. I took it hoping to discover I had some really neat gift not yet recognized or realized. I was hoping for a gift like healing or prophecy or interpreting tongues or preaching like Billy Graham or Chuck Swindoll. But where did I score the highest? In administration! *"Oh thanks God. I get to do the paper work for these other folks who get to do far more important and exciting things."* Needless to say, I was not pleased nor did I appreciate the results of this test.

I fumed for awhile, as people do when told some truth about ourselves we don't want to hear.

But then I remembered that administration is one of the gifts listed in the Bible. (I Corinthians 12:28) God must have thought it was important to the building of His Kingdom or He wouldn't have included it as one of His gifts, would He? Who was I to tell Him it wasn't important? Then I thought about all the jobs I had had, jobs I really enjoyed and could do well: jobs that required organization, keeping good records, keeping track of details, balancing books, keeping things neat, tidy, in good order. Give me a cluttered, dirty closet, attic or garage, add in a couple of hours (or days) and let me go to work. Throw in a pair of rubber gloves, a bucket of water, cleaning supplies, a trash can, some shelving and plastic tubs...and look out! As stupid (and un-fun) as this may sound to most of you, I enjoy a challenge like that. In fact, I'd rather do that than make phone calls! Organizing, pitching, and categorizing stuff floats my boat. (It's not *all* I like to do, but it seems to be something I was born with...or perhaps gifted by God?) Doing these things comes naturally and easily for me. But not all the gifts God has given me have come naturally or easily.

Chapter 14

As I said earlier, speaking in public is not one I would have requested and has been extremely difficult to believe in and put into practice.

I was the kid who had the same Sunday school teacher for 1st and 2nd grade. Once I missed a Sunday because I was sick. My teacher came to our house and brought me a coloring book. Naturally, I said, 'Thank you' as I had been taught. Then my teacher, with a very surprised look on her face, turned to my mother and said, "I didn't know Barbara could talk." Obviously, I hadn't spoken one word in her class for two years of Sundays. Rather shy? That was me.

During my senior year of high school, a friend asked if I would like to work on the yearbook. They needed someone to organize the photos and write quips under the candid shots of our senior class. It was a job with my name written all over it, but one I would never have applied for. Since I didn't have to interview for it, I said "Yes!" I enjoyed the job immensely, though you can tell from what happened at Christmas that I still wasn't opening my mouth very often. (The job didn't require much talking and that was fine with me). The students and teachers on the year book staff exchanged names for Christmas gifts. I received a poem from the yearbook advisor who had drawn my name: "Your taste in clothes is quite superb. Your winning smile choice. But in three months of working here, I've never heard your voice." See what I mean? I was seventeen years old and still not talking. (To my kids, grandkids and current friends: this is pretty hard to believe isn't it? I seem to be making up for lost time). The fact that I am invited to speak to people about my faith in Jesus continues to surprise me. When people quote something they heard in one of my messages years before, I am astounded. Knowing they heard something from the Lord that impacted their life from one of my talks continues to humble me.

The only reason I can now stand before people and speak is because I finally said "yes" to God about an area of my life where I had sworn, "No, never." One day after going through another struggle, but also knowing God would be with me through it, I said to Him, "Do whatever You need to do so I become the woman You want me to be.

Chapter 14

Use me anyway You see fit." That's a pretty gutsy thing to say to our Creator who can do anything He wants. But I also believe He would like all of us to tell Him just that.

When we get serious about being all God wants and needs us to be, we can <u>discover</u> the gifts He has given us, <u>accept</u> them with a grateful heart, and then <u>use</u> them as He intends them to be used. No one has all the gifts, yet all the gifts are needed for the building of God's Kingdom here on earth. To be spiritually healthy and doing the Lord's Will, we need to exercise our gifts and appreciate the gifts of those around us. As individuals, communities, churches, and countries, we desperately need this. So I implore everyone to discover, accept and use whatever gift or gifts you have been given. Whether you are extremely comfortable, or scared to death, run with them! Thank God that He devised a plan to give each of us gifts as He decides. And do you know the special blessing of doing what He asks? He blesses us back in ways we never imagined! And, in addition, He never asks us to do anything without empowering us to do it. What a God. What a

Savior. What a Friend.

As I've said, we all need to exercise the gifts God gives His children. And the last thing we need to do is be jealous of each other's gifts, as I was for some time. That's like the big toe saying to the elbow, "I'd rather be an elbow. I don't like getting stuffed into panty hose and pointed shoes or thermal socks and stiff work boots every day!" Ever stub your big toe and realize how much you need it to be where it is so you can walk without limping? Or imagine the heart saying to the earlobe, "Boy do you have it easy. In the last 24 hours alone, I've had to beat 103, 680 times…pumping blood through this entire body to keep it alive. *And you?* You just hang there and let people decorate you with pretty things. Man, I'd much rather be an earlobe!" Our bodies would be a mess if our parts switched places with another part because they thought they would be more appreciated or useful some other way, wouldn't they?

The same is true for the building of God's Kingdom. Each of our gifts are important to the total functioning of the whole. Each part needs to do the job it was chosen to do, or the whole

Chapter 14

body suffers. So the next time we think another person's gift is more special than ours, we need to remember the lesson of our big toe and earlobe. "Would I want them to be or do something else? Or do I need them to be what they are, where they are and doing what they do, so I look somewhat normal and can function normally too?"

Chapter 15

I was fortunate to be raised in a loving household, but it was also one where all compliments were deflected or denied because if we accepted them, we would probably become conceited. And conceited people were yucky. But do we need to apologize or deny it when someone gives us a compliment on a gift we've received? I don't think so. I realized that when my daughter and son-in-law gave me a beautiful Angora sweater one Christmas. Every time I wore it to church, at least a dozen women would ask me to give it to them when I got tired of it, something I couldn't see doing in my lifetime. Would it have been wrong to tell these ladies that it was a gift from my kids? I can't imagine why it would be. The sweater was a gift chosen especially for me by people who love me and wanted to give me

Chapter 15

something special. Wasn't that a wonderful thing for them to do and wouldn't it make sense to tell those who commented on it that it was a gift from my children? The same must be true for the gifts God gives us. We must use them and thank God for the gifts He gives us.

When people ask me what I did before I retired, I am happy to tell them. I have no problem sharing my back-ground in business, writing, and even single-parenting. But I usually cover my mouth and mumble, 'sometimes I speak too'. Why is that? I don't think someone is conceited when they tell me they play the piano or lead a choir or paint pictures or are a doctor. So why can't I be thankful, instead of feeling it would be pompous, to say, "God also allows me to occasionally speak for Him." It is because I am afraid of "thinking of myself more highly than I ought" and thus become conceited. Such thinking, however, means I am ignoring the rest of this verse which says "but rather think of yourself with sober judgment in accordance with the measure of faith God has given you." (Romans 12:3) Why do I try to hide this speaking gift from my Heavenly Father? This gift was chosen for me by God who knows me better and loves me more than anyone else. The same God who created the Universe wants His message, His will and His love shared with others through my voice. How awesome is that? Isn't it wonderful that He chooses ordinary people to do His extraordinary work? That means there is hope for all of us....no matter how "ordinary" we feel.

It is also wrong to apologize for our gifts because we belittle the giver when we do. If you have the gift of hospitality, enjoy making and serving coffee for people at church, bless you. If you open your home when a need is expressed for temporary housing for someone having a rough time, bless you. If you stop along the highway and help people change their flat tires or jump start their engines, bless you. If you knock on doors and tell people about the difference Jesus has made in your life, bless you. If you visit the sick, send notes of encouragement, bake cookies or casseroles for the single mom or the widower down the street, bless you. If you sing or play music, or paint pictures that move and inspire

Chapter 15

people, bless you. If the Lord has blessed you financially and you share your resources with those who are less fortunate, bless you. If you have any skill that is beneficial to others and you use it to help someone in need, without thought of a reward, bless you. And if you have been called to speak the gospel so that others may hear His marvelous Word, bless you too! If I had never received more than the wonderful gifts of children, health, faith, *and* administration, I would feel most highly blessed among women. Yet He added more than I ever dreamed or hoped for. Since He was willing to do it for me, He is willing to do it for you too.

Whatever our spiritual gifts and talents are, God gave them to us to use for the benefit of others. So let's discover them! Rejoice in them! Thank God for them! Then go out and use them and let God have the glory for the great things He will accomplish *through* us because we've said 'yes' to Him.

Will you pray with me.............

Dear Heavenly Father, no matter how hard I try to convey how awesome You are, the words in the English language just aren't adequate. Thank You for explaining who You are, not just with words, but through the life, death and resurrection of Your one and only begotten son, Jesus Christ. Thank you for Your gift of salvation, freely available by believing and accepting Your Son and what He did for us. If that was Your only gift to us, it would be far more than we deserve. Yet You didn't stop there. You have given each of us other gifts too. You sent us an example to follow so that others may see who You are and how we should live. You also entrusted Your story into the hands of us~~~mere mortals, everyday ordinary people who sin and disappoint You and ourselves on a regular basis. How could You believe that as human as we are, we could handle such an assignment? It must be because You promised to come into our lives and do Your work through us. Whatever Your reason, Lord, we thank You. We are honored to have been chosen to carry the mantle of faith from this generation to the next in whatever way we can. We shall try

Chapter 15

very hard not to let You or them down. Help us to accept with gratitude and use with utmost care the gifts You have given. Let us be bold enough to let other Christians know that they too have been gifted and have a responsibility to You and to us to put these gifts to good use. We stand before You a humbled people. Give us the courage to go out and do what You have called each of us to do. And I know that if we wait until we have perfected Your gift, we will never get started. Help us step out of our comfort zones by taking risks and leaving the results to You. Help us to trust Your Word more than ourselves. In Your precious name, Amen."

Chapter 16

*B*ecause I don't speak "off the cuff," I have a file drawer filled with the messages God has prompted me to write. Each one contains at least one lesson from the Lord. Contrary to what I thought for awhile, all spiritual growth does not have to come through pain, although it seems most of mine did. I would not want to relive some of my experiences but I also wouldn't trade them for all the tea in China (or all the Reese's peanut butter cups either, which I like much more than tea). God knew what it would take to make me truly His. I can never thank Him enough. That He was able to take some of my foolish choices and unfounded beliefs, stay with me through the consequences, and continue to love me, use me, and *want* me, is still amazing. *What do you do with a God like that?* <u>Accept</u> the gift of His son,

Chapter 16

Jesus Christ, who paid the penalty for every sin we have committed and ones we still will. <u>Live</u> in His forgiveness, acceptance and love. <u>Serve</u> Him by telling others our stories in hopes that they too will take this God into their hearts and learn the difference He will make in their lives. Why settle for a life of quiet desperation when He offers a rich, fulfilling, abundant life for all of us?

If some of my struggles teach anyone an important lesson about God or yourself, I pray that you learn it through reading His word, rather than by stumbling into many pits and wondering if and where God fits into your life. If you ever wonder, "Why was I born?" "What is the meaning of life?" "The world is full of millions of people so how can God, if there is one, possibly know or care about me?" "If God exists, does He really love me?" "What does the crucifixion and resurrection of Jesus have to do with me?" "Does this Jesus really want to be involved in my daily life, not with just the big things, but the little ones too?" If you've ever asked yourself any of these questions, I hope this book will speak to you. I pray that your journey isn't as painful as mine has been.

But I also pray that one day you will be able to say, "Do whatever it takes, Lord, to make me the person you want me to be." Then stand back and watch which valleys you not only survive, but grow through in the process. Valleys that the "old you" never could. The miracles will flow as He takes you from valley to mountain peak and back again. And hang onto Him tightly all the way because it will be quite a ride!

I pray the day will come, when you can say the same as the writer of Psalm 40: 1-3.

> "I waited patiently for the Lord;
> He turned to me and heard my cry.
> He lifted me out of the slimy pit,
> out of the mud and mire;
> He set my feet on a rock
> and gave me a firm place to stand.
> He put a new song in my mouth,
> a hymn of praise to our God.
> Many will see and fear
> and put their trust in the Lord."

Chapter 17

Probably the hardest lesson for me to learn has been "How do I dump the fears that paralyze me?" Did you know that "Fear Not" is in the Bible more often than "Love Me?" Doesn't that speak volumes about how well God knows our human condition? Since childhood I have been afraid of anything that might cause physical pain. Swing on the monkey bars? No way! I might fall and get hurt. Ride a two-wheel bike after I had fallen down on my first try and bloodied my knee? No way! So I put the bike away figuring I would try again the following summer. I did. I had the same results. It wasn't any fun, so I quit. It took me three summers to learn to stay on my bike and discover the thrill and the freedom of pedaling through our neighborhood with the summer breeze on my face.

Sleep on the upper bunk? No way! Both my brother and sister had done that, fallen out, and had to have stitches in their chins. This was not for me either! Why bother if you were going to get hurt? (For a few years I waited to see how I would end up with stitches in my chin, thinking it was some rite of passage I would have to endure during my childhood). Try out for the school choir or swim team? Not this girl. I would have to do a solo audition and never had the nerve to try. What if I made a fool of myself and they turned me down? My mother told me frequently that the worse anyone could do was say, "no," but for some reason I never wanted to take that chance.

I continued to live in my self-made, protective shell many years. I kept it on during college and even into my marriage two years later. It still concerned me that if people got to know me, they would discover there really wasn't much to know. So I made very little effort to cultivate friendships. Besides, at the time I had a loving husband and mom for friends. *Who needs more than that?*

Somewhere in my early 40s I attended a seminar where the following quote opened my

Chapter 17

eyes to the poor way I had been living for Christ: "Courageous faith will take you places that mere belief will not." I had been trying to live my faith but was in no way doing it courageously. How can God use a person who holds back from doing anything other than what they can do comfortably? We may do some things well, but never as much as God created us to do. One of my on-going fears has been that, when I meet God face-to-face, He will say, "Oh Barbara, I had so much more for you, but you wouldn't let go of your doubts and fears." I needed to learn the difference between <u>mere beliefs</u> and <u>courageous faith</u> and see if this difference affected my journey with God.

Is there a difference between what we believe and how we live that out with courageous faith? Yes indeed. Someone with *belief* responds this way to the tight rope walker who is asking for volunteers to climb on his shoulders and cross Niagara Falls with him: "Oh I'm sure you can do it...I'll just stand here and watch." *Courageous faith* however says, "Oh I'm sure you can do it. In fact, I've seen you do it. I'll climb on your shoulders and we'll cross the falls together." Would

I ever volunteer for something like that? No way! Yet after joining the single's ministry, I did things that scared the heebie-jeebies out of me. Thankfully, I've lived through them to see and share some of the majesty of God's creation. I learned some life lessons along the way too. I can't imagine how much I would have missed of God's beautiful world if had I continued to say "no" to any opportunity that had the potential (in my mind) of causing pain. I liked keeping my feet on the ground where I felt I was in control of whatever happened. It's kind of funny that so much of my life was spent trying to prevent getting physically hurt. Little did I know that when I was twenty-nine, a doctor would say to me, "You have experienced more pain than most people do in a life time." That alone should have taught me how useless it is to fear what might happen in the future. I wasn't in control after all and never would be.

Chapter 18

In reading the Bible, I discovered several people who *did* live their faith courageously. Perhaps you've heard the story of a kid named David. David was the youngest of eight brothers. When the Israelites, who were God's chosen people, were called into battle against the Philistines, the older seven brothers went to fight while David was left home to tend the family's flocks. One day David's dad told him to go to the battle, take a sack lunch for his brothers and see how they were doing. When David got to the battlefield, he was surprised to discover that no one was fighting. There was just one really big guy yelling taunts at the Israelite soldiers. God's chosen people were huddled in fear, trying to figure out what to do about a giant named Goliath, who was over nine feet tall and a very experienced warrior.

David asked what the scoop was and found that Goliath had been coming out of the enemy's camp twice a day for 40 days and nights threatening, intimidating, badgering and mocking King Saul and his army. "No sense having a big bloody battle, Goliath yelled, "just send out your finest warrior and the two of us will fight. Whoever wins will be the conquering side." Sounds simple and fair enough, right? Yet no one was willing to take on this challenge. Saul stood a bit over six feet tall and was by far the Israelite's best soldier, but was afraid to fight Goliath. Instead of looking up and remembering Who was on his side, Saul was concentrating on the size of his enemy and was scared silly. I find this is a mistake a lot of us make. We concentrate on the giants and circumstances of our lives instead of looking to the One who has promised to be with us through anything and everything. I heard recently that "if He brings you to it, He will also bring you through it." And I say "Amen" to that.

When David heard the taunting of Goliath he thought, "Wait a minute. What's wrong with this picture? Are we not God's chosen people and

Chapter 18

hasn't He promised that He will deliver us from all our enemies? Why am I seeing only fear in our soldiers rather than faith that all God's promises are true and that He will deliver us from this enemy too?"

David approached Saul and told him he would fight Goliath. Can you imagine the snickering this created? *"A 14-year-old kid challenging a nine foot giant? Give me a break."* But David finally convinced Saul that he had killed both lions and bears with the Lord's help and the Lord would help him now. So Saul agreed to let this young boy do what no soldier would. Saul tried to get David to wear his battle gear, but David found it too heavy and cumbersome. So he said "no thanks," got his sling shot out of his hip pocket, gathered five smooth stones and went to do battle with the giant. (I Samuel 17)

Saul had <u>belief</u>. He was a Godly man, chosen to be King of Israel by the Lord himself. But when push came to shove, it was a 14-year-old shepherd boy who had <u>courageous faith</u>. David not only believed, he acted on his belief, saying, "Lord, this is your battle. I go in your name. I'm fighting for your reputation. I want you to be glorified today." So with a home-made sling shot, a few pebbles and an unshakeable faith, David faced the giant and, well, I suggest you read the book to discover "the rest of the story".

I've faced a few Goliaths in my life. But mine are not usually tall, hairy and ugly. Most of them are little voices in my head saying, "nah nah nah nah nah...nah nah nah nah nah." Nagging voices repeat nagging things to me, over and over again. Unfortunately I often fail to realize that none of these negative voices are from the God who made me. Does this sound like Him to you? "If you try that, you'll fail. If you risk that, you will look dumb. If you do that, you'll fall, get hurt and embarrass yourself. And if you dare try that, you'll prove once again how incapable and uncoordinated you really are." No, these voices were not from God, but they were the ones that ran through my head. I was truly loved, accepted and cared for at home, so I'm not sure where these thoughts came from. But they had the power to keep me paralyzed for almost forty years and still do from time to time.

Chapter 18

Fear of failure with a capital "F" is my biggest giant. But it wasn't always so. There was a time in my youth when I thought I could fly. (No airplane needed). I practiced by jumping from the top railing of our back porch, again and again. I jumped as high as I could. I flapped my arms like a bird. I wanted so badly to do something that hadn't been done by anyone else. Did I prove I could fly? No, I landed on the ground, just like every kid who has ever tried it.

When I was eleven we moved to a new house with a basement. I still wanted/needed to do something that would prove to me that I had a little coordination and fearlessness, so I decided to take a flying leap off our basement stairs. I walked down to the fourth step from the bottom, swung my arms real hard and pushed myself into the air! I was doing great until my forehead collided with the I-beam that ran down the middle of the ceiling. As I lay in a heap at the bottom of the stairs, trying to hold back the tears of both pain and embarrassment, I made a vow: *"Never again, Barbara, never again will you try something new and different. You have proven for all time that it just doesn't work for you."* At the ripe old age of eleven, I settled down to live a sedentary life. Can you imagine? How foolish and how limiting was my decision. Adventure, risk taking, being brave was for people born with an "S" on their foreheads for "Super-Star." But it wasn't for me with an "F" for failure on mine.

Is there anyone who can identify with me? Do you have giants in your life too? Is there anything holding you back from being all you want to be and doing all you want to do? Why is it so hard to believe that the One who said, "I have come in order that you might have life---and life in all its fullness" meant it for us?

Thank goodness I've yet to see any of my dozen grandchildren live like their fearful grandma. They are smart and brave and able to express themselves, even to adults. They try new things and are encouraged by their parents to do so. Both my kids and *their* kids have learned that the only way you will know if you can do something is to try it and keep on trying until you master it! My youngest grandson learned to ride a two-wheel bike when he was five. (Remember, I didn't

Chapter 18

conquer that until I was ten). I'm so proud of Landon, but more importantly, he is proud of what he has accomplished. Gaining a healthy confidence in oneself as a youngster is a very good thing!

Chapter 19

When I read Chuck Swindolls's book, <u>Quest for Character</u>, I discovered that many exceptional people *became* exceptional because they didn't make excuses, even when they had legitimate reasons to do so. Here's a list of excuses from his book and what some exceptional people did about theirs:

<u>"Are you letting a physical handicap hold you back?</u>

…Strike him down with infantile paralysis and he becomes Franklin Roosevelt.

…Burn him so severely that doctors say he'll never walk again and you'll have a Glen Cunningham who set the world's one-mile record in 1934.

…Call him a slow learner and retarded and you'll have an Albert Einstein.

Chapter 19

...Deafen him and you'll have a Ludwig van Beethoven.

Are you letting your background/your heritage hold you back?

...Raise him in abject poverty and you have an Abraham Lincoln.

...Have him or her born black in a society filled with racial discrimination and you have a Booker T. Washington, a Marion Anderson and a Martin Luther King Jr.

Are you letting present circumstances hold you back?

...Lock him in a prison cell and you have a John Bunyan
...Bury him in the snow of Valley Forge and you have a George Washington."

Then there is Corrie ten Boom, Joni Erickson Tada, Michael J. Fox, Chuck Colson and countless others who haven't let the cards they were dealt, or the poor ones they chose to play, determine what they would accomplish in their lives. Let's face it. Once we give our lives to Christ, we have no excuses that can stop us from becoming all He wants us to be. We need to tell our fears to take a hike. How can we rationalize and justify not leading a life that makes a positive difference in this world when we have a God who says: "For I am the Lord, your God, who takes hold of your right hand. *I will never leave you nor forsake you.*" (Hebrews 13:5b) The writer of Hebrews also declares and we can say with confidence, "The Lord is my helper; I will not be afraid; what can man do to me?" (Hebrews 13:6) We need to remind ourselves of these verses and the promises they hold whenever our fears start messing with our hearts and minds. *God is on my side... what can mere men do to me?* What should we do with a God like that in our corner? How do we handle the promises He makes to us? Will we believe Him enough to climb on His shoulders and let Him worry about how impossible our situation appears? Or will we maintain our attitude of fear, doubt and worry? If we honestly believe

Chapter 19

He is strong enough to support us *and* our giants, we will live a healthier and fuller life.

Chapter 20

Some marvelous opportunities came my way while I was on the staff of the singles' ministry that the "old me" would have passed by. And even though I still shook and doubted myself when presented with these adventures, the new me decided to walk through these "Doors of Opportunity." In the process, I discovered some truths about God and myself that I would have missed had I continued to say, "No thanks."

In 1992, our ministry planned a vacation to a dude ranch in Colorado. I was very excited and said "yes" when asked to be the staff representative on this trip. We would spend a week at the ranch, ride the same horse every day, swim in their huge pool fed by hot springs (which eased any sore muscles we might get from riding), eat home-made meals three times a day, and go for

Chapter 20

a hayride. There was even a cookie jar in the kitchen which was daily filled with fresh-baked chocolate-chip cookies. What wasn't there to love! The first five days of the trip were great. Then it was time for our last, all-day ride, which would take us to the top of a 12,000 foot mountain.

A man from our ministry had made this trip before and told us it was a beautiful ride. But he also said that there was a very narrow path on the trail where the mountain wall was on one side, a sheer drop off on the other, and just enough room on the path for the horses to walk single file. This "sure to be frightening spot for people who don't like heights," was about 30 feet long. The fact that I had been given the tallest horse on the ranch (which I couldn't get on without help), and the fact that I never liked heights, just about convinced me that this was a ride I would skip, gladly.

Everyday others (knowing my fear of heights) would ask, "Are you going on the all-day ride?" I didn't want to miss the opportunity to see something I might never see again, but that horrible spot on the way down really had me terrified.

I woke up the day before with a sore jaw from grinding my teeth all night and with a knot in my stomach from just thinking about doing it.

You get the picture. I am a very slow learner when it comes to dumping all my fears. It dawned on me I didn't know if Bob, who had already made this trip twice, was going again this time. So I approached him with, "Knowing what you know and having fears similar to mine, are you going on this all-day ride?" His response? "Oh absolutely... and you have to go too." "But Bob, you said you were terrified." "I am," he replied, "but I'm going anyway." I finally decided that if someone who could relate to my fears and knew exactly what we were facing, was taking this ride, something must happen on the mountain that was worth the risk. So I signed up to go.

It was a three-hour ride to the top and the scenery was phenomenal. We ate a sack lunch above the timberline that overlooked the Continental Divide. There were mountains and valleys as far as the eye could see. After awhile, some threatening clouds started rolling in, so the ranger decided it was time for us to head back

Chapter 20

down. By this time I wasn't talking to anyone except my horse, God and myself. *This is it... here we go...oh God, what am I doing up here?* I didn't know where this particular, death-defying ridge was. We crossed over several ridges that I hoped "were it" because they really weren't too scary after all. I kept patting my horse, Rollins, and whispering in his ear, "what a good horse you are." Then we rounded a curve and all doubt left my mind whether this was the spot or not. There was no place to go...except forward.

I gripped the reins tightly but let Rollins have his head, as we were instructed. Then we stepped out on the ridge. I looked up, I looked out and I looked down. The mountain side was sheer rock, except for some fingernail scratches (were these Bob's, I wondered?) Other than that, I felt and saw only one thing. It was beautiful, awesome, spectacular, overwhelming...there aren't enough stupendous words in our language to describe it. Miracle of miracles, it was everything but frightening! *"How could that be? How could that happen?"* I didn't understand it at all but I enjoyed it immensely. Later on I remembered

Psalm 34:4: "I sought the Lord and He answered me; He delivered me from all my fears." I had read that verse many times but this was the first time He delivered me so miraculously, so completely, so quickly. Conquering that mountain pass in Colorado was probably a once-in-a-lifetime experience. It is certainly one that showed me, yet again, "Take God at His Word and see what He has for you."

Like David with his five pebbles, I went to the top of the mountain as prepared as I could be. Not like David, however, I took my fears with me. Up until that week I had spent maybe five hours on a horse and always on flat ground. But by the day of this last ride, I had spent one solid week with one particular horse and had probably been on his back for a total of fifteen hours. Because of the training and the fifteen hours of experience, by Friday I knew several things about Rollins that I hadn't a clue about on Monday:

1. He could slip or stumble on a rock, but he had no more desire to fall than I did.
2. He would stop occasionally just to catch

Chapter 20

his breath and there was no moving him forward until he was ready.

3. Whereas some horses kept on walking as they relieved themselves, Rollins always stopped for his bathroom break. It took me awhile to realize what was happening, but once I did, I didn't worry about getting too far behind the horse in front of us. We would catch up when Rollins was done with his business.

4. After hearing a sound numerous times that I thought was a bug attacking us, I turned around and found it was only Rollins swishing his tail. I relaxed.

5. Horses have personalities, just like we do. Rollins liked some of the other horses and some he did not. He didn't like to get too close to those he didn't like and he let me know which ones those were. After realizing this, I smartened up and didn't try to force him to keep pace with the horse ahead of us if he didn't want to; after all, he had the right to choose his friends just like we do.

Spending quantity and quality time with this one horse increased my trust level of him immensely. As I later shared this experience with a friend, telling her I had gone to a scary place with a horse I trusted, she said, "Do you realize what you just said? Isn't it the same with God?" Actually spending more time with God will help us know His character better and we'll learn to trust Him more? What a concept! This revelation was surely a gold nugget of wisdom to add to my saddle bag.

When we spend time with God, we not only learn about His character, we also learn His ways and His love for us. We discover He can be trusted with every aspect of our lives. "In this life you will have trouble," is one of God's warnings to us, but He concludes that warning with a promise, "but take heart, I have overcome the world." (John 16:33) When we stay connected with the God of the Bible, we can know Him as He truly wants to be known and say with confidence, "I can do everything through Him who gives me strengthen." **(**Philippians 4:13) After experiencing what happened on that mountain

Chapter 20

trail, I thought I would never let fear paralyze me again. Unfortunately, I'm not that wise.

I still have a small handful of fears that I keep tied around my waist like a little boy with a bag of marbles. But I do know that He is able and willing to deliver me from my fears when I release them to Him. If I'd stayed at the ranch that day, rather than riding up the mountain, I would have missed not only some of God's majestic handiwork, but also one of His lessons and promises to me. Are you missing something important because your giant is bigger than your God? Do the "nah, nah, nah, nah nah" voices in your head continue to control you? Please, let them go. And learn with me that **courageous faith** in our God who has made countless wonderful promises to us, will take us places that **mere belief** never will.

If I never ski in Aspen or jump out of an airplane, I don't think the Lord will be disappointed in me. But if fear keeps me from being His disciple and witnessing to His truths, He will be greatly disappointed. If fear of self and what others might think, keeps me from doing all He has equipped and empowered me to do, I will miss countless blessings set aside for me in His warehouse. And you will too if you allow the giants in your life (poverty, illness, handicaps, abuse, shame, guilt, circumstances, family history, etc.) determine your future for you. When we spend time with God every day, our trust in Him grows, deepens, and enriches us. We will be able to continue trusting Him, our firm foundation, even when we go through tribulations which are part of life on planet Earth.

Chapter 21

My week in Colorado taught me another important lesson about God and my misconceptions of His character. On an afternoon when some folks chose to go to a rodeo, the rest of us decided to blaze a new trail at this Waunita Hot Springs Ranch in Colorado. One of the owners led us through a wooded area where banks and banks of blue flowers bloomed among the aspen trees. The path looked untraveled, at least so far that season. The flowers had been blooming for some time, but the odds that anyone had seen them were very slim. And I thought, *What's the point of being so beautiful if no one is going to see you?* Obviously these flowers weren't worried about that. They were blooming for one and one reason only: because that's what they were made to do. They weren't worried if they were noticed or not. They didn't waste time thinking, "What if a horse tramples on me? What if someone picks me and I die? What if we don't get enough rain to keep us blooming? What if the plant next to me gets bigger and brighter petals than I do? Why wasn't I born an aspen tree so I could see the mountains above and the valleys below?" *Whine, whine, whine.*

They'd been created by God to do one thing: "bloom on one of My mountains and let Me take care of anything or anyone who comes against you." We were blessed that day by their beauty which was the direct result of their obedience to their Creator. Granted, they weren't given a choice, as we are, but since even the waves are stilled at His command, wouldn't we be wise to learn something from nature? Is anyone being blessed by our inner beauty because of our obedience to do what God has asked us to do? Does it really matter if anyone notices our good works or not? Shouldn't the fact that God knows be enough? I believe so.

Another time I was privileged to take an Alaskan Cruise. As usual, there were "side trips" to sign

Chapter 21

up for before we left. Some of my friends were going to take a helicopter ride and they wanted me to come too. Those who signed up would fly to the Mendenhall Glacier, get out, and walk around on this huge block of ice that was thousands of years old. I almost let my fear of heights (and flying) keep me back. But then I remembered the day I went to the Continental Divide on the back of Rollins, so I plunked my money down and signed up to go.

Was my stomach churning as we put on our life jackets and glacier-walking boots several weeks later? You betcha! In addition, the man who had promised to hold my hand through the ordeal had been assigned to another helicopter. The flight to the glacier wasn't too bad, although I told the pilot I thought he had banked his flying machine too far to the left (being the wise, back-seat driver that I was). The walk on the ice was great and none of us fell into one of the gaping cracks. But I was shocked when the pilot said that those who sat in the back seat on the flight over (where, of course, I had been, usually with my eyes closed) should sit in the front seat on the flight back to the ship. I hesitated and almost backed out because the front window ran from above our heads all the way under our feet! *Was he crazy?* But what happened as we took off and flew over another of God's masterpieces? All I saw was beauty... mountains, valleys, rivers, sky, almost too much to take in. I reminded myself again what I would have missed if I had given into my fear of heights and having no control. I've looked back on my life and considered all the things I have missed because of a preconceived idea of "what might happen" instead of trusting the God who made me. I waited over 40 years to learn this, but I'm glad I wasn't 80!

Since then I have ridden in a cable car dangling several hundred feet off the ground in Israel. That was the only way we could visit King Herod's "never to be conquered" fortress on Masada, built before the time of Christ. This fortress sits 1300' above the Dead Sea. (In other words, it was a long way down). Yes, I held someone's hand during the cable-car ride, but I did it! A group of us also swam in the Dead Sea and discovered that the salt can hold up our physical bodies as well as

Chapter 21

God holds up the earth. I've even slept overnight in a tree house with my two youngest granddaughters. (And discovered it's a long walk to the bathroom in the middle of the night). But it was worth every minute and a few aches and pains to listen to the crickets, wonder about the raccoons that might join us, read a bed-time story by flashlight, and whisper prayers with these precious children while a blanket of stars twinkled overhead. (If you've never tried it, I strongly recommend it.)

When given the opportunity to white-water raft on a #3 and #4 river with two other grandchildren last summer, I immediately signed up and never felt a quiver of fear. We had a ball. Maybe I'm finally learning that life is short and there's no time like the present to do as much as I can, while I can.

Chapter 22

Early in my walk with Christ, I was more interested in reading the New Testament than the Old Testament because it seemed more relevant to my life in the 20th century. Jesus had come and fulfilled all the prophecies of the Old Testament, so why not just go forward from there? But then I realized that part of the richness of the Old Testament was the fact that God didn't just use perfect people to accomplish His purposes. What if He had? What hope would there have been for any of us? At one point, I felt that God wanted me to write a message about these non-perfect people and the decisions they made to obey Him, whether His request made any sense or not. I sat down and wrote, "Is God Still Asking His People to Do Stupid Things?" As I reviewed the Old Testament stories, I was amazed

Chapter 22

and amused at the people God used and what seemingly stupid things He told them to do. The beauty of these stories is that, contrary to us who can read the whole event, these people did not learn the results of their obedience until *after* they had obeyed God. (And we won't know the outcome of our choices to obey His instructions until *after* we obey either. That is why "Trusting and Obeying" are so important in our walk with Christ.)

When God saw that the earth was rotten to the core, He told Noah (the only righteousness man He could find) to construct a big boat because He had decided to destroy the whole earth with a flood. But God wanted to save Noah's family and some animals, thus the command to build a boat. God told Noah exactly how big it should be and what materials to use. Noah's neighbors laughed at him because he was building a huge boat miles from any water. How would he get it to the river? What a fool to waste his time and money on that monstrosity! But Noah did as God commanded and a week after the ark was completed and fully loaded, the rain began. "And Noah did everything just as God commanded him." (Genesis 6:22) For forty days and forty nights, "all the springs of the great deep burst forth, and the floodgates of the heavens were opened." (Genesis 7:11b) The people had laughed while Noah built the ark, but it wasn't a laughing matter when they drowned in the flood. After the rain stopped and dry land appeared, Noah's family and the animals could finally get off and settle on dry land. God promised that He would bless Noah's family and never destroy the earth that way again. He even gave them a sign of this promise. When you see a rainbow, remember that is a reminder of God's promise to us and be grateful.

Then there was Abraham who was instructed by God to leave his home country, take his family, herds and possessions with him and "go to the land I will show you." (Genesis 12:1b) Did Abraham say, "Wait a minute...how about a map so I don't get lost? And it really would give me some peace if you told me our destination."

No, Abraham just trusted that God knew what He was doing and so he packed up all his stuff and started on a journey that would take 40 years to complete. I've heard that this trip to the Promised Land could be done in a matter of days, even with thousands of people, sheep, cattle and goats following in a caravan. So why didn't God take them directly to their destination? Because He knew there were lessons the Israelites needed to learn before they arrived and it would take awhile for them to trust Him. They were also a stubborn lot, like many of us. So they traveled and grumbled and ate manna and traveled and grumbled and ate manna. Some generations died, new ones were born. They went round and round until God decided to let them out of His waiting room and led them to Canaan, the land He had promised.

Do you ever feel you've been sitting in God's waiting room long enough, wondering if your prayers will ever be answered? After all, 40 years is a LONG time to wait for anything. Some people kept their faith in Abraham and God and learned their lessons well, even living long enough to tell their kids and grand-kids their story. Some complained, doubted, and decided they had a better plan, but they didn't make it across the desert alive. An expression I believe I read in Sue Monk

Kidd's book, <u>When the Heart Waits</u>, has helped me through tough times of waiting for God to respond to my prayers. I believe her book is where I read the expression, "Who you become while you wait is more important than what you achieve." Can you get your heart and mind around that? Who you become *while you wait* is more important than what you achieve? This means God is much more interested in our character than He is in our accomplishments. Yet often we forget that, get mad during our waiting period, and decide "I can do this without God" and go our own way. The results are never as wonderful as if we had waited for God's timing.

Then there was another word to Abraham, "Hey man, you're going to have a baby. Yes I know both you and your wife are way past making this happen. But trust Me, I can!" It didn't happen for several years, but always as good as His word, Sarah became pregnant and son Isaac was born. Another far-fetched, yet true event, took place when Abraham was told to offer his only son as a sacrifice to God. Did Abraham do what most of us would in a case like that? "No way---this is

Chapter 22

my only son and we waited over 50 years to have him. No way will I kill him." No, the man of God took his son Isaac, a knife, a couple of servants, wood for building an altar, and ascended the mountain where God told him to go. Although I'm sure his heart was breaking and his mind kept saying, "This makes no sense; I must have gotten the message wrong; this isn't even fair; I've done everything God has asked me to do and this is my reward?" Yet despite his doubts, despite his fears, he obeyed. Abraham built an altar and laid his son on it because, as crazy as this seemed, Abraham trusted God with his whole heart. Obedience to his Holy Father was even more important than the life of his precious son.

Sounds pretty rough, doesn't it? But when God saw that Abraham trusted Him enough to obey even this senseless (from a person's perspective) instruction, He sent an angel to stop the hand holding the knife over Isaac's body. The angel said to him, "Now I know that you fear God, because you have not withheld from me your son, your only son." (Geneses 22:12) Abraham was severely tested by God, but proved beyond any doubt that he was a true believer. Each time we obey, God will bless us and take us to a higher level with Him. Will the Lord ask you to do something that sounds ridiculous by our world's standards? I hope so. And I pray you obey. Over and over again the Lord asks ordinary people to do impossible, unbelievable things---will you be one of them?

Another famous man in the Old Testament was just a kid when he was deceived by his brothers and thrown into a pit to die. But Joseph was rescued, sold as a slave, and then promoted to the King's castle. Later he was thrown in prison for a crime he did not commit and left there for 14 years. Because of his goodness to another prisoner, he was finally released and became second in command to the King. He then had the wisdom and the authority to do something that saved thousands of people from starvation. How would you like that to be *your* story? The end sounds great, but what Joseph endured before that would be tough for anyone to handle. Joseph persevered and received more blessings than he could number.... trusting and honoring God through the all the years of misunderstanding, lies and deceit.

Chapter 23

The introduction to the book of Judges in The Life Recovery Bible states, "The book of Judges shows what happens to a society when their citizens do whatever they choose. The people of Israel refused to learn from their past mistakes. They refused to follow the path of freedom by obeying God's plans for righteous and healthy living." The quote continues, "The same is true for us today: we have refused to learn from history's lessons by doing things our own way. Then, as now, doing things our own way leads to enslavement and suffering; following God's ways is the only way to true freedom." Sounds like America today, doesn't it?

Have you read the newspaper or watched the news lately? I believe, and many others do too, that our nation is reaping the consequences of turning our backs on God and going our own, selfish ways. I remember hearing another expression that sums this up quite well. "If God does not punish the United States of America, He will have to apologize to Sodom and Gomorrah for destroying them for their wicked sins." Ouch!

Another seemingly stupid order came from God when He told Moses to take his staff and put it in the Red Sea so that the waters would part. This would allow the Israelites to escape from their slave owners, who were chasing them, by crossing the sea on dry land. Sound preposterous? Certainly! Did Moses do it? Yes, he decided to obey God's command. Did it work? Read the book of Exodus to discover anew the miraculous results that can happen when we are brave enough to take God at His word.

Gideon, another man of God, tried to take his 30,000 soldiers into battle when God told him to cut his army down to 3,000 men. He was then told to go fight against 10,000 of the enemy soldiers. Foolish, down-right stupid you say? Not when God is involved. If Gideon's army had won the battle with their 30,000 soldiers, they would

Chapter 23

probably had given themselves all the credit. But when they won the battle with only 3,000 men, they learned that "with man this is impossible, but with God all things are possible." (Matthew 19:26) Have you learned that yet? It's another toughie to hang onto, but when Jesus is in control, the results are astounding. (Has anyone ever told you that you + God = a majority when you are following the will of God?)

Consider Joshua who led the Israelites after Moses died. His army was preparing to conquer the city of Jericho when he received this word from the Lord, "March around the city once with all the armed men. Do this for six days. Have seven priests carry trumpets of rams' horns in front of the ark. On the seventh day, march around the city seven times, with the priests blowing the trumpets. When you hear them sound a long blast on the trumpets, have all the people give a loud shout; then the wall of the city will collapse and the people will go up, every man straight in." (Joshua 6:3-5) Talk about an illogical, seemingly impossible command! Just walk around the city a few times, blow your horns, give a loud shout and fortified walls will fall down? Who in their right mind ever heard of such a thing? Yet Joshua had learned that God could be taken at His word. So Joshua did what the Lord commanded. And guess what? The walls collapsed and the Israelites walked in and captured the city.

Have you ever read these stories and thought about such seemingly ridiculous requests? Will you be counted among the fools who do what God commands? Try it and discover what He has in store for you.

Chapter 24

For over 30 years I believed that if you had a god who worked for you, that was fine. I chose Jesus, others chose Mohammed, or Hitler, or Buddha or others who claimed to be god. And still others choose gods of their own making: money, fame, power, 'stuff', etc. Who was I to tell anyone that there is only one true God? Wouldn't I be arrogant if I believed and tried to tell others that there is only ONE WAY to get the fullness of life Jesus talks about *plus* forever life in heaven with Him?

Thankfully, when I was questioning what kind of God I had given my life to, a neighbor asked a question I had never been asked before: "Do you believe the Bible?" I responded with, "Well, the parts that make sense I do, but the parts that don't make sense, I don't." Her question and my answer stayed with me for several days. Finally I had an insight that led me to believe that the Bible is 100% God's word to us. My thoughts ran like this: "Would the Creator of the Universe leave a book that was half true and half false and expect us to figure out which was which? Could there be more than one Creator who lived and died to make it possible for us to have a relationship with Him?" The answers to these questions were an absolute *NO*. So I had a big decision to make: believe it all...or *not at all*. As Vance Haver says in <u>Pathways</u>, a devotion book by David Jeremiah, "The Word of God is either absolute or obsolete."

I choose to accept it all on faith that there is only one, true, living God. Who else could have put His inspired word into forty different men over a period of 1500 years and have it stand the test of time? What other all-time, best- selling book in the world is as relevant to our lives today as it was to the folks who lived when Jesus did? Once I made the decision to accept the Bible as all true, His Word started making sense in ways it hadn't before. It became a "light unto my path"." <u>He</u> said, "I am the way, the truth and the life.

Chapter 24

No man comes to the Father except through me." (John 14:6) So am I arrogant or intolerant when I say there is only One God? No, I'm just repeating what the Man said, *"I am* the way, the truth, the life..." If you believe He was just a good teacher, great prophet, or nice man, He must also have been insane to make the claim that He *was* God.

Imagine Peter walking on water. Have you ever tried it? I doubt it. Or if you did, you got all wet in the trying. Yet when Jesus told Peter to get out of the boat and walk towards Him, Peter believed it could happen, so he did it. Everything was going fine until Peter took his eyes off Jesus, looked down, and saw the turbulent waves rolling beneath him. That's when He got scared and started to sink. I can think of many times when I looked at my circumstances, became overwhelmed by them, took my eyes off Jesus, and began to sink. Why do I forget that I have trusted my life to the Man who said, "a righteous man may have many troubles, but the Lord delivers him from them all." (Psalm 34:19) I've learned the hard way that the brain can only hold one thought at a time. We can trust Jesus for the outcome of our situation or we can worry ourselves into a state of panic and illness. When I am wise, I choose the former, trusting way. When I concentrate on what is happening to or around me, instead of Him, I lose every time. My worries have a way of attacking my body and that can happen to you too. Headaches, back aches, tummy troubles, sore muscles, ulcers, being overweight or even underweight are often the result of what is going on in our heads. My physician once told me, "Only about 10% of the people who come to me really need a medical doctor. The rest need a counselor instead." Wise words from a wise woman.

Chapter 25

One of the most profound things I heard from Him (come to think of it, has He ever said anything that *wasn't* profound?) woke me in the middle of the night and kept me awake 'til dawn. For at least two years I had read that Ken Davis, nationally-known Christian writer, speaker and humorist, also hosted Dynamic Communicators' Workshops for "wannabe speakers." Each time I heard about these conferences, butterflies would start to dance in my stomach and I would think, "Someday...maybe *someday* I'll be able to attend one of these conferences. Wouldn't that be a really super blessing?" I had heard Mr. Davis speak and thought that attending one of his conferences would not only be a wonderful experience for me, it would also train me to be a better speaker. But I lived in Michigan and the conferences were held in Colorado. The cost of the seminar, including room and board was $795, about $780 more than I had. So I dismissed the idea until God woke me up that night.

Want to know what His crazy idea was for me this time? "It's time for you to attend this conference you've only dreamed about. This is how it will happen: you will ask for financial help." As with other things He told me to do, I argued with Him. I told Him that, once again, He had chosen the wrong person for the job. I reminded Him that as much as I wanted to help others, I would never become a missionary because they had to raise their own support by asking family and friends for money. No way would I ever do that, no way at all!

When God wants to get my attention by asking me to do something I've never done before, He has a way of hassling me until I agree. (The thought of God hassling or nagging anyone might not sound like your God. But occasionally His persistence… *even for my own good*…feels like it to me.) The thought of asking for financial help to attend this conference was a real emotional drain, and

Chapter 25

one that would not go away. It lasted for several days. He wanted to know if, once more, I was willing to obey His idea, even when it gave me goose bumps, knocking knees, and rocks in my stomach just to think about it. I finally had the nerve to ask a couple of friends what they thought of the idea. Surprisingly, they gave me a 'thumbs up' and many encouraging words. One even said that refusing to ask for help was only pride getting in my way and I should "get over it." So I started formulating a letter to send to my friends because it was easier to express my request in writing than to ask people face-to face.

I wrote to those who had heard me speak, were moved by it and said it had helped them on their own faith journey. I not only asked for financial support, but more importantly, I asked for their prayers. I didn't want their money if they didn't pray and believe that this was something God wanted both of us to do. If it wasn't from Him, I wanted no part of it. The response was overwhelming. Twenty loving people sent more than twice the amount I requested. So my airfare and other expenses were also covered. Another lesson of getting my pride out of the way and listening to that still, small voice was received through this action of obedience. Although the verse in Luke 6:38 refers to what we give away, I also think it applies when we give our obedience to Christ: "A good measure, pressed down, shaken together and running over will be poured into your lap." That's what He did for me. The love, prayers and financial support of family and friends were pressed down and poured into my lap!

Be warned: Never tell God, or yourself, what you will never do! I have said "I will never pay more than a $1 for a gallon of gas, never ride in a helicopter, never be a single mom, never go to church without wearing panty hose, never live in Florida, never speak in public, never pray out loud, and especially, never be divorced." I have had to eat all those words and some didn't taste very good. How can we display His power if we only do what is comfortable for us? Sometimes, no matter how scared we are, we have to get out of our comfort zone if we truly want to know how trustworthy He is. (However, I don't believe He asks people to

Chapter 25

jump off cliffs, drink poison or allow a snake to bite them to prove His existence. There is a line between wisdom and stupidity.)

Chapter 26

*I*n John 16:33b, when Jesus said to His disciples "In this world you will have trouble," He wasn't threatening them or us. He was just being truthful. We live in a fallen world (one that has turned its back on God) and there is no way to avoid it, no matter how good we are. Notice that He did not say, "Maybe you'll have trouble." He said we would! Until I was about 20, I believed that if you played fair and behaved yourself, life would always be fair to you. But it isn't necessarily so! We need to learn and teach our children and grandchildren that life is not fair. But God is, always. We need to hang onto this truth, especially when we have no visible proof that He is working in our life.

If we will not, by faith, believe that the whole Bible is true (including the parts where God has

Chapter 26

whole towns, even babies killed), we will never learn the whole of God's character. He loves us, He is kind, He is merciful, He is gracious, He is forgiving, but He is also just. "Do not take revenge, my friends, but leave room for God's wrath, for it is written: 'It is mine to avenge; I will repay', says the Lord." (Romans 12:19) Those who refuse to believe that Jesus is just and allow Him to deal with the people who have hurt us and those who deny Him, miss out on knowing Him as He fully desires to be known.

In the New Testament God tells a man to go ahead and marry his fiancee even though she is pregnant. (It used to be shameful to be with child and not married.) Joseph had to believe the angel who spoke to him, telling him what no other man has ever heard: "Yes, Mary is pregnant. And yes, she is still a virgin. You have been chosen to be the earthly father of the Messiah that your people, the Israelites, have been praying and waiting for, for hundreds of years. It's a big job for a big man, but I know you can handle it. Continue to love Mary and the Lord with your whole heart, and just watch what He can do." So Joseph did what he was told to do and will always be remembered as the man who had to believe the impossible: his bride was truly a virgin, yet she was going to have a baby. And not just any baby, however, but the Savior of the world.

The ultimate test of faith and trust came when God told the most unreasonable of all things to His only begotten Son, Jesus the Christ. "Let people ridicule and reject you, belittle and beat you, strike and spit on you, and take your robe along with your reputation. Let them laud and then laugh at you. You must submit to thorns on your head and nails in your hands and feet, but do not complain. In fact, forgive those who torment and torture you. Let them drain your strength along with your blood. You are to accept the cruelest form of torture man has ever developed and then you must die. You see, my precious One, because I am not only a loving God, but a just one, someone must pay the price for all the sins of all the people who have ever lived and those yet to come. As unfair as it seems, the sins of the whole world will be laid on your back. This price can only be paid by someone pure. And you

Chapter 26

and you alone are the only pure and perfect creature on earth. I know it probably sounds insane, but I also know you believe me when I say, 'I will raise you up again'." *One to pay the price for millions?* What a ridiculous, totally unfair plan...yet the only one that could satisfy our holy God.

Would we give up our only child (or any of our children) to be killed in order to pay for another's sins? I think not. But God did. Have you ever fallen to your knees and thanked Him for this incredible sacrifice in order to have your sins forgiven? In doing so, did you receive the assurance that you can spend eternity with Him? Our lives are full of choices every day. But the most important choice we will ever make is deciding to take God at His word and invite Him to live in and through us. He takes the incredible and makes it possible. Take Jesus at His word and see what an abundant, adventure-filled life He has in store for you.

Chapter 27

As I mentioned before, more than once God has asked me to do some seemingly impossible thing that made no sense at the time. But when I obeyed, I was blessed. Do I follow His lead all the time? Oh that I would! I taught many lessons on how to let God be in control of our lives, but I wasn't smart enough to practice what I preached in every situation. Sometimes I thought I was smarter than the lessons I learned and had taught. How arrogant. How foolish. And, oh, the price we pay when we ignore His warnings.

I made a god of my first husband and lost him. A stiff lesson, but one I needed to learn. "You shall have no other gods before me." (Exodus 20:3) I was truly convinced that I could not live without this man. Yet something he said as he left turned out to be true: "You'll be better off without me." It

Chapter 27

was years before I would admit that to myself. I waited three years for him to come to his senses and come back to us. For ten years I listened, read and even shared some of the stupid things people do when they fall in love and decide to marry a second time. (Sometimes when your heart thinks it is in love, your brain falls out your ear.) That happened to me.

A new minister came to town. He wasn't tall, but he had dark hair and was handsome. He immediately took an interest in me. As before, I was awed to be chosen over at least 40 available single women in our small community. I had told God sometime before this, "If you want me to marry again, you'll have to put the man on my front porch because I'm not wise enough to choose who would be best for me." Right after I started dating this man, guess what? He would appear on my front porch about 6AM and offer to take our dog for a walk. Through rain and ice and sleet and snow, he appeared all smiles with his dog and took ours with him before his busy day began. What a guy!

Many experts in the field of divorce and death

have written that people should wait *at least two years* after the loss of a mate before getting serious about anyone else. This man had only been divorced a few months. But since I had been single for ten years, I reasoned that some of my long-time singleness could be credited to his short time of being single. (Guess my reasoning fell out with my brain.) Once again I was swept off my feet and fell in love. But this time I forgot everything I had learned during my many years of being single. Red flags? What were those? I saw some things that bothered me, but we both worked in ministry and we loved the same God. Didn't that make us an exception to the two-year rule? Certainly the things I heard, read and taught didn't apply to *us!* Granted, he had a few personality traits that confounded me because I had never experienced them before, but I made excuses for them. He was very busy with many important responsibilities. He also had a special place in his heart for the lonely, hurt, sick and dying. He made hospital calls in the middle of the night and home visits a real priority in his life. The elderly, widows, widowers and those who

Chapter 27

were ill loved him dearly because he would visit them and listen to their stories, week after week. Didn't that alone mean he was a really nice man?

Two months after we met, he asked me to marry him. Because of some signs I looked for (in addition to showing up at my front door), I thought God was giving me permission to say "yes." A date was set for just six months later. Every time I would get an uncomfortable feeling in my stomach about our relationship, I would beat it down with a stick. *You've waited a long time. You might never get another chance. His family is thrilled that he found you. No matter what, we can make it work if we keep Christ at the center of our lives. We really haven't had much time together, but that's because of our careers. Once we're married, we will have more time to learn some important things we still don't know about each other.* I ran this litany through my head as often as necessary to keep believing it. Our wedding plans moved forward.

To his credit, when I expressed my doubts about us getting married so quickly, he agreed to call off the wedding for awhile and wait until

I was sure. But by then over 200 people had received invitations. People were so happy for us. Arrangements had been made, rooms reserved, food ordered. It would have been far too embarrassing for me to call it off at this point. And so we wed. (I have since counseled women that, if their gut is telling them something is wrong when they are walking down the aisle, they should turn around and walk back out.)

Less than 24 hours after saying, "I do," I found myself waiting over an hour for him in the lobby of the hotel. I was crushed to realize that I had made the biggest mistake of my life. My new husband was on the phone upstairs checking in with the church office to see if everything was running smoothly and everyone was following his instructions. It was just one indication that his job was more important than his bride, even on the first day of our honeymoon. It felt like he had captured me and now it was time to get back to his real life. I don't mean to sound selfish, but one of his cousins called with a personal problem. They both believed that he was the only one who could help her through it. So he spent at least

Chapter 27

an hour a day on the phone with her every day of our two-week honeymoon. One of the pastors who conducted our wedding had told him that he was "a man and husband first, and a minister second". I'm not sure he ever understood what that meant. Although it isn't fair to label people, I finally found some words to describe the things he did that hurt so much: compulsive, obsessive, manipulative, controlling things. He truly believed that there was only one way to do anything: his way, the *only right way.* I frequently felt that he believed I had just gotten off the boat from a far away land. Even though I had managed a home, had a meaningful career, raised three children, and impressed him for several months, all of a sudden I didn't know the right way to lock a car, a good place to leave my keys, the best way to shop, the right discipline for my youngest child, when to make our bed, and so on and so on. He didn't like conflict, so He rarely corrected me to my face. He just left notes on the kitchen cupboard telling me what I had done wrong that day or going behind me and re-doing what I had done to "make it right."

After two years of this and his agreeing that "next time" I could do something that he wouldn't correct, he would turn around and do it his way anyway. Do you know how often this can happen before you feel utterly useless and invisible? Even though I had survived my first-failed-marriage without professional counseling, I knew that the two of us would keep going round and round, pooling our own ignorance, and never moving forward unless we got some outside help. Where does a woman go when she knows the consequences she is suffering are due to her own foolish, life-changing decision? How could I seek help without destroying our reputations? Who could I tell what I was going through? Share with someone at work? *Heavens no.* That was where I had been taught all the things I should have considered before marrying a second time, all those things I felt "above". Speak to someone at church? *Gracious no.* What would they think of him and of me? Weren't we both Christians? Wasn't that enough to hold our relationship together and make it work? No matter what we looked like to others, I knew our marriage was not honoring

Chapter 27

God. The grief of knowing that hung over me like a big, dark cloud.

I finally found the name of a woman therapist who I decided to try. When she walked in for my first appointment, I knew immediately she wouldn't be able to help me. She was tall, thin and pretty. Just the opposite of how I felt. Immediately I convinced myself that she wouldn't be able to relate to me at all. I judged her knowledge, character, and abilities on her appearance alone. By the end of the hour, however, I discovered she was the real thing: intelligent, wise, compassionate, and non-judgmental. I saw her for four years, continuing to believe that *somehow* we could make this marriage bearable and turn it into one that would please both God and us. I knew we were failing miserably, although to everyone else, we seemed to be okay. I also knew that I could never leave him because being divorced once was bad enough. Going through a second divorce was unthinkable for someone who thought of herself as a Christian.

During my fourth year of counseling, my husband agreed to come with me. Through our joint conversations with the therapist, we made a list of guidelines to implement into our marriage. These were things we both agreed to do or *not do* in order to ease the tension I felt at home. They worked, sort of, for awhile. Then, after he had done something I had begged him not to do, and which he had agreed in counseling not to do, he said, "Well, I didn't like those rules anyway." He was never physically abusive, but the things he did gave me an assortment of physical and emotional pains. It's amazing to me how our bodies attack themselves because of what is going on in our minds.

After a few counseling sessions, my husband stood up in the middle of one and announced that he was leaving and not coming back. He felt he had heard enough and spent enough of his time on the issues that were tearing me apart. How do you reach someone when they cannot or will not listen to those who care about them? More than anyone, I wanted this marriage to work. After six years, however, I reached a point when I felt only three options were left to me: 1) Numb out. Don't think. Don't feel. Become a non-person;

Chapter 27

or 2) Admit myself to a mental institution; or 3) Die. Sound melodramatic? Probably, but those were the only choices I felt I had left. So strong was my belief that I could never leave him, I had already decided that I would have to pretend to be a grieving widow if he passed away before me. In actuality, it would feel like a ton of pain I had been carrying for 20, 30 or 40 years had rolled off my back.

Chapter 28

Several months later, as I was preparing for a woman's retreat, a voice in my head said "You could leave." I jumped, knowing that was never an option for me. I already felt like a hypocrite for preparing a talk on the reality of Christ when my own life was such a mess and I felt I had blown it with God forever. The idea of leaving our marriage was preposterous, so I knew it hadn't come from me. "*Oh Lord, you know I can't. We both love you; I can't admit to such an error. How will my children feel about their 'supposedly-Godly mother' who made such a foolish mistake? Our friends, our church, our family…what heartache, confusion and disappointment leaving him would create.*" Yet, again the voice came, "You could leave."

I had absolutely no desire to go through another divorce. I just realized that if we stayed

Chapter 28

together, we would continue going up and down on the same roller coaster, never getting anywhere, and never able to get off. I needed to get away for awhile, some place where my husband couldn't affect what I did or thought each day. Someplace where I could clear my head and try to start thinking like an intelligent, mature human again. I made a list of what I would need and appreciate in a temporary home. Naturally, first and foremost, I would have to afford it until we got back together, which I assumed would happen. Since the church had provided my home and utilities for six years, this would be my biggest challenge. The thought of moving out of our house gave me feelings of hope, yet also dread. I felt so badly for setting such a poor example for my children of what a Godly marriage should look like. But my counselor assured me, "You are not to be the example they are to follow. Jesus is."

I was hoping I could find a place closer to work in a safe neighborhood. What God led me to, I knew I didn't deserve. It was everything I had hoped for, and so much more: the rent was $10 less than I budgeted. It had a fireplace, its own laundry facilities, garage space, and a second bedroom I could use as an office. There was a lovely and loving landlord, who knew my situation and attended the church where I worked. True to her word, she kept her silence about my situation, for which I was very thankful. I even had a deck, trees, flowers and a creek, right outside the door wall which provided my private entrance. I knew I was unworthy to have such a wonderful place. I had told God it would be easier to move into a hut than to continue living the double life I had been, both at work and at church, for six years. Yet this place is where He led me.

"*You can't! You shouldn't! I have failed both you and myself,*" I cried to Him. He found this place for me anyway. I walked most nights through all kinds of weather, in our lighted, gated community. I prayed like never before. I cried like never before. (Even though I thought I had cried myself out over my previous failed marriage.) *What have I done now to ruin my life? Why did I marry him when my gut was telling me something was wrong with our relationship?* I mentally and spiritually beat myself over and over again. Many

Chapter 28

times I wanted to step off the path and vomit into the bushes all the garbage I had accumulated in my gut. Sometimes praying was so difficult that instead I would try to sing, "Jesus loves me, this I know, for the Bible tells me so." Over and over again, desperately trying to believe it could possibly still be true for me.

I thought I had learned what God's grace meant through other people's experiences, but discovered I hadn't a clue about grace until Jesus blessed this repentant sinner that year. I also realized I had a lot of pride that needed to be dropped at the foot of the cross. After healing from the loss of my first marriage, I had vainly thought, "Okay, I understand you now God. Sometimes bad things happen to people because they need to learn just how real, available, powerful and loving you are. I realize I didn't know how real my faith was until I was put in the fiery furnace where my world was turned upside down and inside out. Thank you, God, for this lesson. I can take it from here."

Boy, who did I think I was? One night as I was out walking I covered my face with my hands and admitted to God, "I'm going to need you *every day* for the rest of my life! Can you handle that?" I'm sure He chuckled, then reminded me that was the reason He came into my life in the first place. He knew I would never be wise enough to live out His plan for me without spending time with Him on a regular basis. And you know what? None of us are. Think of it. Our best relationships exist because we have spent considerable time with certain people and let our hearts become transparent with them. We will never get close to anyone until we are willing to share our hurts, fears, disappointments, mistakes and failures. If that is true with people, why would it be different with the God who created relationships? I needed to share the real me with God just like I had learned to do with a few people. I needed to listen, learn, trust and obey Him before I would ever attain the abundant life He has promised to His children. It's quite enlightening to know we can share deep, hidden things about ourselves with Him and a few select people and still be loved and loveable. Granted, God already knows our thoughts even before we think them, but He

Chapter 28

wants us to talk to Him about these things we have tried so hard to keep a secret. He knows that will be the start of our healing.

Several weeks after moving out of the parsonage, my husband asked when I was coming back. I said I didn't know yet and it didn't seem that anything had been resolved between us. He even told me that when I came back, everything would be the same as it was before. He had been asked to make a five-year commitment to pastor another church in the local area, but wasn't going to go there if I couldn't tell him when I was joining him. Because I had not seen any improvement in our relationship, I could not give him a date. So the next day he notified his District Superintendent that he wanted to transfer back to the state where his folks lived. His request was granted and he moved almost 1000 miles away. How do you work on a relationship with someone who lives that far away and has no intention of changing his behavior so that his wife could stop hurting? Realizing we were husband and wife in name only, I filed for divorce several months after he moved. By then we had mutually agreed to dissolve the marriage. It was the hardest decision I ever had to make. Contrary to what I thought my future was destined to be, I didn't have to wait thirty-some years for that ton of pain to start letting go of me. I still had much to face, but I felt more whole when alone than when I was married. I was very sad that our marriage ended this way. It seemed so unthinkable, but I was getting divorced for a second time. There were now two Ds on my forehead. I was so humiliated and so ashamed. I felt I would have to live in seclusion and I knew that God would never be able to use me again.

Only because of His goodness, forgiveness and grace, God eventually proved me wrong about this too.

Chapter 29

When we have grown beyond knowing that being a Christian means more than being an American who goes to church, we need to answer this question: "*How* has knowing Him changed my life? And if not, *why not?*" After I had asked God to come into my life and take over, I felt very different inside. I felt refreshed, reborn, and able to live with a whole new attitude knowing that there truly was a loving God who knew me and all my faults and came to live with me anyway. I thought for sure others would notice this "changed Barbara." Much to my disappointment, no one did. I couldn't understand it. Why couldn't anyone see the differences in me? I decided the changes would have been more visible if I had been a criminal, a drunk, or a really nasty person prior to accepting Christ. But I had been raised not to be any of these. The quiet, polite, usually kind person was all anyone could see after I accepted Christ and she wasn't much different than the "before me." I tried talking to my family about asking Christ into my life and how I felt so differently, but all they could say was, "But we believe in Jesus too." I couldn't understand why they weren't as excited as I was about falling in love with Him. When we fall in love, don't we want everyone to know?

If our thoughts, words, attitudes or actions are no different after we accept Christ than they were before, what is the point of asking Him into our hearts? If what we do in our free time, the books we read, the music we listen to, the movies, programs, and Internet sites we watch, are no different after accepting the one true God, again I ask, what was the point? If the friends we hang around, the way we feel about those who have hurt us, and the amount of time we spend with God and other believers, hasn't increased or changed, then I question whether we really have personally met Jesus.

I heard on the radio recently that "God will

Chapter 29

bring or allow crises in our lives so that He can take us to a deeper understanding of Him and His character." If I had known that when my life was going from crisis to crisis, would I have believed it? Probably not. But if I had, perhaps I wouldn't have shaken my fist at Him and cried out, "I don't *want* to know you any better if the only way I can grow spiritually is through one more crisis. Enough is enough already. Please stop!" Thankfully, with the wisdom that only He has, He didn't respond to my cry as I wanted Him to. When He wants to do a work in us, which can only be for our own good, we need to let Him do it whatever way will work: through a blessing or yes, sometimes through a crisis.

It's a fact that either we will be transformed by His presence in our lives, or we don't really have Him in our lives. We may have believed in God and prayed to Him for years and years, but have we met His son Jesus? I believe that unless we spend time alone with Him, read His story, look for the answers to life's questions in His book and believe, by faith, that the Bible is 100% His inspired Word, we can't know God, His son or the

Holy Spirit as they desire to be known.

Most of us look for something or someone to fill the empty spaces in our hearts that will make us completely satisfied. It has been said that there is a "God-shaped hole" in all of us and until we fill it with Him, we will never be satisfied. We look for fame or wealth or popularity or new toys or another person to complete us. Yet this hole can only be filled by the One who created us, has loved us since the beginning of time, and has been with us through every valley and mountain experience we have ever had, whether we knew it or not. Only God has the power and the wisdom to provide what we really need, what can truly satisfy.

And what we really need, the only One who can fulfill us, is the Person of Jesus Christ. He wants to live in each of our hearts. He is waiting to be recognized, waiting to be called upon, waiting for us to realize that without Him, there is no life of meaning or fulfillment, no lasting peace, no sense of purpose, no hope for our future. I think sometimes He cries to be known by us just as He certainly as He died for us.

Chapter 30

When Christ comes into our lives and inhabits our hearts, what does He find? I think the parable in Matthew about the seed, the soil and the sower speaks to all of us. To help explain His mission on earth, Jesus frequently told parables that the people of His time could understand. By telling these parables, He made word pictures that all could relate to, if we give them some serious thought. Most of us probably didn't grow up on a farm, but this parable about seeds and the soil can speak to us about our hearts... even if we were raised in a concrete jungle.

Seeds grow according to the soil in which they are planted. And we grow according to what soil Christ finds in our hearts. In this parable, the farmer is God and the seed He plants is His word. I'm sure many are very familiar with this parable, but sometimes if we've heard a story many times, we really don't "see it" as it was meant to be seen. Strange as it may sound, I move my household furniture a couple of times a year...not because it *needs* to be moved, but because I have stopped seeing it after it sits in the same spot for several months. Once I move it, however, it becomes fresh and I see and appreciate it again.

Like my furniture, I heard the bible story of the seed, (from Matthew 13:1-23) so many times that I was familiar with it. But I didn't understand it as it needs to be understood until I read Phillip Keller's book, <u>A Gardner Looks at The Fruits of the Spirit</u>. I learned the following important principles from Mr. Keller's book.

Mr. Keller explains that, just like the farmer knows that every seed will not produce a plant, God knows that His word, when we hear or read it, will not always produce what He wants. The soil represents our hearts and the four different types of hearts where His seed (the Word) can fall. Which type of soil, or heart, best describes where you are with Him now?

There is the hard soil that represents the cold

Chapter 30

heart that won't receive Him. No matter how often a seed is thrown on pavement, it will not grow. Some people are like seeds thrown on pavement: no matter how often they hear His word, it never penetrates their hearts because Satan snatches it away. Mr. Keller states, "Perhaps more often than anything else, the ground of our persistent old thought patterns is the toughest soil He has ever had to tackle." If you were raised in an environment where only negative things were said about God, you probably grew up believing them. I believe this hard path also represents those who just accept what they heard in Sunday school without ever questioning it for themselves. Perhaps they think, "I don't need to learn any more about Jesus. I heard all that when I was a kid." No room for growth in that heart.

Then there is the rocky dirt. The seed falls between the rocks but there is not enough soil to take root, so it sprouts quickly and then dies. These seeds represent people who fail to think things through on their own. Their lives are run by the crowd, doing whatever happens to be "in" at the time. Did you wear a big cross around your neck and a WWJD bracelet just because it was popular for awhile? Have you stomped your feet and waved your arms because the other people in church were doing it? Do you read all the self-help books that are on the market because Dr. Phil or Oprah recommend them? When we base our faith on these things, our faith will fade as soon as the fad does. Mr. Keller says this about stony, rocky soil: "Any point or any place in life where a person prefers to disobey God, to go his own way and do his own thing, is stony soil."

If you've ever planted a garden, you know that sometimes there is also thorny soil, which is full of weeds. This represents hearts that hear and believe God's Word, but don't change because the culture has more influence on them than Christ does. This happens when we let our energies, time and resources (the nutrients that allow the seed to grow), take over and allow them to run our lives. Thorny people get lost in the weeds. The Word dies before it bears fruit. According to Mr. Keller, this can also be called the Cluttered Heart. We have so many interests and take on so many responsibilities that the most important

Chapter 30

Person in our life gets crowded out. It's even possible to fill our life doing good things and not recognize the One who has given us the ability to do these things! "By faith in Christ we must believe that He actually can take the waste land of our lives and transform it into a garden for God." And we are never so 'weedy' that God gives up on us.

Were there thorny people in Jesus' day? Of course there were. And, unfortunately, many of them spent their lives in the temple thinking they were pleasing God because they lived by all the rules and ridiculed people who didn't. What was the thorn that choked the Word of God from the Pharisees? Tradition. *Tradition!* If we go to church and do nice things because that is the tradition we were raised with, but never come face-to-face with our loving God, we truly miss out on the abundant life He promises.

In Matthew 13:22 Jesus lists two things that can choke out his Word: the cares of this life and the love of riches. I've never had a true love of money (although I admit having some brings more pleasure than not having any), but I was at the top of the list when it came to worrying about the cares of life. God talks about the foolishness of worry because what can we change by worrying about it? Yet I used to think it was the wife's and mother's duty to worry about things, because if she didn't, who would? I was very good at dragging the struggles and worries of yesterday and the possible struggles and worries of tomorrow into the day the Lord had given me. This pretty much ruined the current 24-hour present He gave me each day.

Being raised in the 1940s and 1950s in America, I somehow picked up the belief that "more is better". My first full-time job after becoming a single parent was for a family that seemed to have everything that could make anyone happy. They owned a thriving business, drove expensive cars, wore great clothes and in addition to having nice homes, they had a second home on a beautiful lake with lots of boats and other big-boy toys to fill their vacation time. Were they happy? Were they content and grateful? *Shouldn't* they have been happy, content and grateful? Because I didn't have these things, I assumed they had "arrived" when it came to reaching the good life. Then one

Chapter 30

day I heard them talking about wanting a home in Europe and it hit me, "what we think is enough will *never* be enough". I learned then and there to be happy and grateful for everything I did have and that has made a huge difference in my priorities. Do I still enjoy buying a new dress or flying out-of-state to see my grand-kids? Sure. But I am grateful for everything I already have and am allowed to do, because of the One who provides all my needs.

Thankfully, there is also <u>good</u> soil, "soil that has been plowed, fertilized, and softened by the rain. This is the soil that has been worked over by the farmer, so that it is ready to receive the seeds and harvest a good crop." And good soil, a tender heart, will produce a crop of whatever seeds are planted 30, 60 or 100 times more than the seeds that went into the ground. One pumpkin seed shrivels up and dies, is planted, and then produces a vine with multiple pumpkins on it! That's how things work in God's economy. One Man died so that millions could spend eternity with Him. We are asked to 'die to self' in order to become what God has planned for us.

When we are ready to receive whatever God has for us, whether it is good or seems terrible, then we will truly have a heart in which He can produce a good crop. He can then make us into the people He created us to be and use us to bring glory to His Kingdom. Good soils, open minds, ready to receive what the Master Gardner has planned, are prepared to hear from Him. They don't become too proud or too busy to listen. They never say, "I am a self-made man (or woman)." After they hear Him, they obey. As Mr. Keller says, "Even the best of soil must first be broken before it can become beautiful." When a whole field is broken up or plowed by the farmer, a beautiful and rich crop is produced. We admire the flowers and taste the delicious fruits and vegetables that are grown. But how often do we think about what had to be done to the soil to produce such a crop? It is the same with people. Those who have given their hearts to God and asked Him to be the main thing in their lives are those who exemplify the characteristics of Christ, which is certainly a good crop! We may never know how "worked over" their lives have been, but we can see Him

Chapter 30

shining through by the way they live. Mr. Keller concludes his message on the soils by saying, "There simply has to be something of the likeness of Christ apparent as proof positive that God is actually at work within."

In another book I read, the author said, "Any garden, left to itself, will become overgrown with weeds. Vigilance and regular maintenance are prerequisites to a beautiful and abundant garden." He goes on to say, "So it is with our inner, spiritual gardens. Dependence, discipline, planning, weeding, cultivation, watering, fertilization, pruning, and vigilance against attacks are all part of the growing and flourishing spiritual life." (<u>Seasons of Prayer in Word and Image</u> by Kenneth Boa)

It can be scary to put our lives into the hands of an almighty and powerful God, especially if we know He is going to work us over. He may plow into our circumstances, churn up our beliefs, upset our status quo, and throw out the distractions and the addictions we have accumulated. He then might add fertilizer (that stinky but helpful stuff) to our hearts. He may take us places we don't want to go. He may cause the trials that are supposed to soften us, feel like a dagger thrust into our hearts. "Who needs it?", we may ask ourselves. To which He replies, "You do, my dear child, you do." Perhaps praying this prayer will help you get started on your path to life and freedom with Him.

"Dear patient and loving Father,

    I come to You with the seeds of my heart having been dropped in many different places. These seeds are my convictions, my attitudes, and my beliefs, right or wrong. They have been shaped by my environment and how I have responded to it. I know You want a healthy, honest, open heart, based on Your Truth, for all of us. I want that too. Part of me has been on the hard-packed, beaten path long enough. If I stay there, I will produce nothing of worth in Your name. After I heard about You at a revival, I became very excited to hear that You truly are the One I was looking for. Unfortunately my excitement did not last. I didn't spend time with You and Your Word so that when trouble came knocking at my front door, I

Chapter 30

kicked You out the back. The little I knew wasn't enough to take root in my life. Finally I realized I needed You back and I attended church on a regular basis. But you know what it is like living in today's world where everything is moving at warp speed. It is all I can do to keep up with my career, my kids, my parents, the mortgage, the grocery bill and current news. I'm also supposed to find enough time to exercise, do comparative shopping, eat right and go to my doctor and dentist on a regular basis, *plus* spend time with You? You do understand, don't you? There just isn't enough time in my days to do it all. You must realize that I don't always have time to read and process what Your Word says. But *I will* find time, I promise. As soon as things slow down a bit, I will be able to concentrate on what You have for me. *Then* I will get to know and serve You better.

Oh Lord, to know that You want me in your Kingdom is an awesome thought. To know you sent your One and only begotten Son to live, teach, and show us what You are truly like, is something I have a hard time wrapping my head around. And then You had Him killed to pay the price for my wrong choices and poor decisions? *What kind of love is that?* I want my heart to be like the good soil. I want to take in all that You have for me so I can become the person You want me to be. I want Your purpose for me to be my highest purpose. I want to be one of Your disciples, willing to risk all for Your sake. Please help me Jesus. Please till the soil of my heart by pulling out the weeds and the worries that consume so much of my time and energy. Fertilize me with the good nutrients that only Your Word can supply until I grow healthy and whole. On the day I meet You face-to-face I want to hear, "Well done, good and faithful servant." (Matthew 25:21). Enter into My presence and My party and enjoy all these good things forever. Amen.

Chapter 31

There are many ways I could conclude this epistle of my journey with Christ....perhaps some of you wish I had done it pages ago. The devil is still whispering in my ear, "your chapters aren't in good order," "no one will get what you've been trying to say," "give it up!" But I'm going to push through those nasty thoughts and get this printed before I die, Lord willing. Believe it or not, there are things I still want to share. But I must stop somewhere. So I close with these few thoughts, quotes and verses that have ministered to me in the past and I hope will speak to you. Thirty-eight years after giving my life to Christ, I still need to remind myself of them on a regular basis.

"I walked awhile with Pleasure;
she chatted all the way;

> But I was none the wiser
> for all she had to say.
> I walked awhile with Sorrow
> and not a word said she;
> But, oh, the things I learned from her
> When Sorrow walked with me."

I don't remember the author, but I've never forgotten the poem. It reminds me that others have learned best in the hard places of life too.

There isn't a promise in His word that we can't take to the bank and get 100% return for our investment in His truths. To those I love and those I have yet to meet, His Word is true and it is meant for you!

Through the seemingly impossible or extremely difficult things God has asked me to do, I have learned countless lessons and still have many to learn. It is my hope that my children and grandchildren learn them earlier in life than I did. It is my prayer that they learn the following truths without stumbling into as many pits as their mom and grandma did:

Chapter 31

His ways are always higher (wiser) than ours.

His plans for our journey may take us places we don't want to go.

Pain is not essential for learning God's truths, but I wasn't wise enough to learn things the easy way. I hope you do better.

We may have to give up our dreams in order to follow His.

He can be trusted with everything, every time.

God is on your side, every day, in every way.

The times you can't see that He is doing anything with or for you, you must hang onto His promises and know beyond any doubting that He is *always* at work in your life.

He loves us with a love that goes beyond anything we can imagine and promises "lo, I am with you always."

Are you living your life for yourself and what you want to accomplish? Or have you chosen the higher, narrower, way? Your destiny, your future here on earth and where you will spend eternity depends on how you answer this question. Choose wisely my family, my friends and those I've never met. Please choose wisely. If you haven't already done so, I pray that you turn your life over to Him very soon. There will come a day when it will be too late.

> "Now to Him who is able to do immeasurably more than all we ask or imagine, according to His power that is at work within us, to Him be glory in the church and in Christ Jesus throughout all generations, forever and ever!" Amen. Ephesians 3:20-21

RESOURCE LIST

1. The Life Recovery Bible, copyright 1992 by Tyndale House Publishers, Inc., Wheaton, IL.

2. Pathways, by David Jeremiah, copyright 2010, by Turning Point for God.

3. Hind's Feet in High Places, by Hannah Hurnard, copyright 1986, by Tyndale House Publishers, Inc., Wheaton, IL

4. When the Heart Waits, by Sue Monk Kidd, copyright 1990 by Harper Publishers, San Francisco, CA.

5. Classic Works of Phillip Keller, "A Gardner Looks at the Fruits of the Spirit." Copyright 1986 by BBS Publishing Corporation, New York, N.Y. 10016.

6. Seasons of Prayer in Word and Image by Kenneth Boa. Photography by Carl Alan Smith. Copyright 1999. Published by Honor Book., Tulsa, OK., 74155

CPSIA information can be obtained at www.ICGtesting.com
Printed in the USA
LVOW060723220113

316626LV00002B/7/P

9 781606 475737